COMPUTERS, INTERNET, AND SOCIETY

Communication and Cyberspace

COMPUTERS, INTERNET, AND SOCIETY

Communication and Cyberspace

Robert Plotkin

Facts On File

An Infobase Learning Company

COMMUNICATION AND CYBERSPACE

Facts On File, Inc.
An imprint of Infobase Learning
132 West 31st Street
New York NY 10001

Library of Congress Cataloging-in-Publication Data

Plotkin, Robert, 1971–
    Communication and cyberspace / Robert Plotkin.
        p. cm.
    Includes bibliographical references and index.
    ISBN 978–0–8160–7753–3 (alk. paper)
    1. Telecommunication. 2. Telecommunication—Social aspects. 3. Cyberspace. 4. Information society.
I. Title.
    TK5101.P578 2012
    303.48'33—dc22   2011005013

Facts On File books are available at special discounts when purchased in bulk quantities for businesses, associations, institutions, or sales promotions. Please call our Special Sales Department in New York at (212) 967–8800 or (800) 322–8755.

You can find Facts On File on the World Wide Web at http://www.infobaselearning.com

Excerpts included herewith have been reprinted by permission of the copyright holders; the author has made every effort to contact copyright holders. The publishers will be glad to rectify, in future editions, any errors or omissions brought to their notice.

Text design by Kerry Casey
Composition by Hermitage Publishing Services
Illustrations by Bobbi McCutcheon
Photo research by Suzanne M. Tibor
Cover printed by Yurchak Printing, Landisville, Pa.
Book printed and bound by Yurchak Printing, Landisville, Pa.
Date printed: February 2012
Printed in the United States of America

10 9 8 7 6 5 4 3 2 1

This book is printed on acid-free paper.

CONTENTS

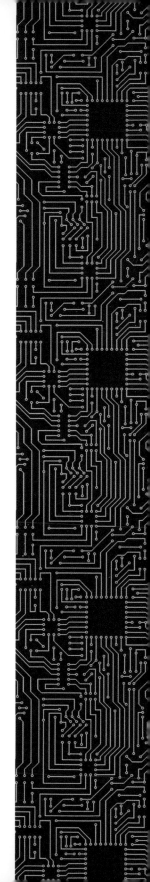

PREFACE

Computers permeate innumerable aspects of people's lives. For example, computers are used to communicate with friends and family, analyze finances, play games, watch movies, listen to music, purchase products and services, and learn about the world. People increasingly use computers without even knowing it, as microprocessors containing software replace mechanical and electrical components in everything from automobiles to microwave ovens to wristwatches.

Conversations about computers tend to focus on their technological features, such as how many billions of calculations they can perform per second, how much memory they contain, or how small they have become. We have good reason to be amazed at advances in computer technology over the last 50 years. According to one common formulation of Moore's law (named after Gordon Moore of Intel Corporation), the number of transistors on a chip doubles roughly every two years. As a result, a computer that can be bought for $1,000 today is as powerful as a computer that cost more than $1 million just 15 years ago.

Although such technological wonders are impressive in their own right, we care about them not because of the engineering achievements they represent but because they have changed how people interact every day. E-mail not only enables communication with existing friends and family more quickly and less expensively but also lets us forge friendships with strangers halfway across the globe. *Social networking* platforms such as Twitter and Facebook enable nearly instant, effortless communication among large groups of people without requiring the time or effort needed to compose and read e-mail messages. These and other forms of communication are facilitated by increasingly powerful mobile handheld devices, such as the BlackBerry and iPhone, which make it possible for people to communicate at any time and in any place, thereby eliminating the need for a desktop computer with a hardwired Internet connection. Such improvements in technology have led to changes in society, often in complex and unexpected ways.

Understanding the full impact that computers have on society therefore requires an appreciation of not only what computers can do but also how computer technology is used in practice and its effects on human behavior and attitudes.

Computers, Internet, and Society is a timely multivolume set that seeks to provide students with such an understanding. The set includes the following six titles, each of which focuses on a particular context in which computers have a significant social impact:

- *Communication and Cyberspace*
- *Computer Ethics*
- *Computers and Creativity*
- *Computers in Science and Mathematics*
- *Computers in the Workplace*
- *Privacy, Security, and Cyberspace*

It is the goal of each volume to accomplish the following:

- explain the history of the relevant computer technology, what such technology can do today, and how it works;
- explain how computers interact with human behavior in a particular social context; and
- encourage readers to develop socially responsible attitudes and behaviors in their roles as computer users and future developers of computer technology.

New technology can be so engrossing that people often adopt it—and adapt their behavior to it—quickly and without much forethought. Yesterday's students gathered in the schoolyard to plan for a weekend party; today they meet online on a social networking Web site. People flock to such new features as soon as they come available, as evidenced by the long lines at the store every time a newer, smarter phone is announced.

Most such developments are positive. Yet they also carry implications for our privacy, freedom of speech, and security, all of which are easily overlooked if one does not pause to think about them. The paradox of today's computer technology is that it is both everywhere and invisible. The goal of this set is to make such technology visible so that it, and its impact on society, can be examined, as well as to assist students in using conceptual tools for making informed and responsible decisions about how to both apply and further develop that technology now and as adults.

Although today's students are more computer savvy than all of the generations that preceded them, many students are more familiar with what computers can do than with how computers work or the social changes being wrought by computers. Students who use the Internet constantly may remain unaware of how computers can be used to invade their privacy or steal their identity or how journalists and human rights activists use computer encryption technology to keep their communications secret and secure from oppressive governments around the world. Students who have grown up copying information from the World Wide Web and downloading songs, videos, and feature-length films onto computers, iPods, and cell phones may not understand the circumstances under which those activities are legitimate and when they violate copyright law. And students who have only learned about scientists and inventors in history books probably are unaware that today's innovators are using computers to discover new drugs and write pop music at the touch of a button.

In fact, young people have had such close and ongoing interactions with computers since they were born that they often lack the historical perspective to understand just how much computers have made their lives different from those of their parents. Computers form as much of the background of students' lives as the air they breathe; as a result, they tend to take both for granted. This set, therefore, is highly relevant and important to students because it enables them to understand not only how computers work but also how computer technology has affected their lives. The goal of this set is to provide students with the intellectual tools needed to think critically about computer technology so that they can make informed and responsible decisions about how to both use and further develop that technology now and as adults.

This set reflects my long-standing personal and professional interest in the intersection between computer technology, law, and society. I started programming computers when I was about 10 years old and my fascination with the technology has endured ever since. I had the honor of studying computer science and engineering at the Massachusetts Institute of Technology (MIT) and then studying law at the Boston University School of Law, where I now teach a course entitled, "Software and the Law." Although I spend most of my time as a practicing patent lawyer, focusing on patent protection for computer technology, I have also spoken and written internationally on topics including patent protection for software, freedom of speech, electronic privacy, and ethical implications of releasing potentially harmful software. My book, *The Genie in the Machine,* explores the impact of computer-automated inventing on law, businesses, inventors, and consumers.

What has been most interesting to me has been to study not any one aspect of computer technology, but rather to delve into the wide range of ways in which such technology affects, and is affected by, society. As a result, a multidisciplinary set such as this is a perfect fit for my background and interests. Although it can be challenging to educate non-technologists about how computers work, I have written and spoken about such topics to audiences including practicing lawyers, law professors, computer scientists and engineers, ethicists, philosophers, and historians. Even the work that I have targeted solely to lawyers has been multidisciplinary in nature, drawing on the history and philosophy of computer technology to provide context and inform my legal analysis. I specifically designed my course on "Software and the Law" to be understandable to law students with no background in computer technology. I have leveraged this experience in explaining complex technical concepts to lay audiences in the writing of this multidisciplinary set for a student audience in a manner that is understandable and engaging to students of any background.

The world of computers changes so rapidly that it can be difficult even for those of us who spend most of our waking hours learning about the latest developments in computer technology to stay up to date. The term *technological singularity* has even been coined to refer to a point, perhaps not too far in the future, when the rate of technological change will become so rapid that essentially no time elapses between one technological advance and the next. For better or worse, time does elapse between writing a series of books such as this and the date of publication. With full awareness of the need to provide students with current and relevant information, every effort has been made, up to the time at which these volumes are shipped to the printers, to ensure that each title in this set is as up to date as possible.

ACKNOWLEDGMENTS

Many people deserve thanks for making this series a reality. First, my thanks to my literary agent, Jodie Rhodes, for introducing me to Facts On File. When she first approached me, it was to ask whether I knew any authors who were interested in writing a series of books on a topic that I know nothing about—I believe it was biology. In response, I asked whether there might be interest in a topic closer to my heart—computers and society—and, as they say, the rest is history.

Frank Darmstadt, my editor, has not only held my held through all of the high-level planning and low-level details involved in writing a series of this magnitude, but he also exhibited near superhuman patience in the face of drafts whose separation in time could be marked by the passing of the seasons. He also helped me to toe the fine dividing line between the forest and the trees, and between today's technological marvels and tomorrow's long-forgotten fads—a distinction that is particularly difficult to draw in the face of rapidly changing technology.

Several research assistants, including Catie Watson, Rebekah Judson, Jessica McElrath, Sue Keeler, Samuel Smith, and Kristen Lighter, provided invaluable aid in uncovering and summarizing information about technologies ranging from the ancient to the latest gadgets we carry in our pockets. In particular, Luba Jabsky performed extensive research that formed the foundation of many of the book's chapters and biographies.

As the saying goes, a picture is worth a thousand words, and this set comes to life through the artwork and photographs it contains. Although computer science, with its microscopic electronic components and abstract software modules, is a particularly difficult field to illustrate visually, artist Bobbi McCutcheon and photo researcher Suzie Tibor could not have matched visuals to text more perfectly.

Last, but not least, I thank my family, including my partner, Melissa, and my dog, Maggie, for standing by my side and at my feet, respectively, as I spent my evenings and weekends trying, through words and pictures, to convey to the next generation some of the wonder and excitement in computer technology that I felt as a teenager.

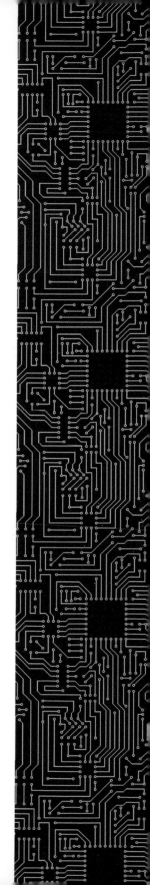

INTRODUCTION

For many computer users, computers have overtaken the written letter, *telephone,* and even face-to-face conversations as a means of communication. In fact, many people use computers almost entirely as communication tools, both because they can now mimic many of the old forms of communication and because they provide new and exciting ways in which to express ideas and to share those ideas. *Communication and Cyberspace* traces the history of communication technology and explores the many ways in which computers and the Internet are now being used to facilitate communication.

Chapter 1 covers the history of communication technology, including the *telegraph,* telephone, fax machine, *radio, television,* and computer. Before the telegraph was invented, communicating with someone just a few towns away could take days, as the message traveled by horse and carriage from its author to its recipient. The telegraph fundamentally changed the way communication happened, since the telegraph was the first technology capable of sending data electrically over long distances via a wire. When Alexander Graham Bell discovered that voice could be translated into electrical signals, he realized that it could be sent across lines as well. The invention of the fax machine allowed pictures, instead of a voice, to be transmitted electronically across the same telephone line. Radio and television also use electronic signals, but without the requirement of a wire. Chapter 1 describes how each innovation in electronic communication led to more complex technologies, eventually culminating in the modern computer, an interactive and interconnected medium of communication.

Chapter 2 examines how staying in touch with other people has become easier with the invention of newer methods of communication. When people lived, worked, and played in small towns, never venturing far from their own homes and communities, there was little need to use technology—even writing—to communicate. This began to change in the Industrial Age, as adults began to work in factories and other facilities outside the home rather than on the family farm, and as even children began to work for a living or reside in boarding schools for extended periods of time. Families and communities became further separated during the great waves of immigration during the late 19th and early 20th centuries. Chapter 2 explores the history

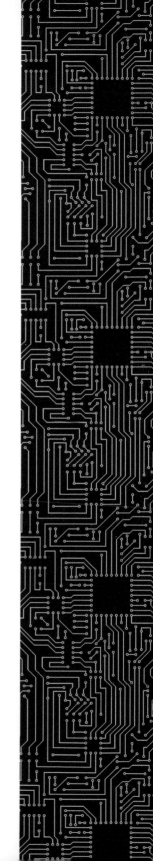

and current state of technologies for enabling personal communication, and the wide variety of ways in which they are being used.

Chapter 3 describes how businesses that need to enable their employees to communicate in ways that advance business goals, with a high degree of reliability, security, quality, and speed, have stayed on the leading edge of developing and adopting new communication technologies that eventually filter down to individual computer users after such technologies become more mature and inexpensive. As more individuals open small businesses, and as even nonbusiness owners seek to market their skills, to publicize their *blogs,* and to communicate with colleagues more generally, the communication technologies that were only available at high cost to businesses just a decade ago are now increasingly available inexpensively online for anyone to use. This chapter examines a few of the particular ways in which businesses have helped to advance communication technology.

Chapter 4 focuses on how schools have modernized some areas while remaining relatively low tech in others. As with all other technological developments, shifting a lesson from print to electronic form may result not only in a change in the physical media through which information is transmitted, but also a transformation in the process by which knowledge is obtained. This chapter explores a variety of ways in which computers and the Internet are changing the face of education.

Chapter 5 describes how publishing and journalism are changing with the advent of *desktop publishing,* self-publishing, and blogs. The Internet has thrown the journalism profession into turmoil. Though newspapers and magazines experimented with online publishing over the years, many attempts have failed. Alternatives to traditional newspapers, such as online editorials by professional journalists, have been popular in recent years. The invention of the Kindle and other e-book readers allows users to write and publish their own books without any investment from publishers, editors, or printers. This chapter discusses how publishing changed as restrictions on who could publish were removed by modern technology.

Chapter 6 discusses of how technology can be used to accommodate people with disabilities. Technologies such as *speech-recognition* software, special keyboards, non-keyboard text-entering devices, and eye-tracking technology allow people to overcome disabilities and not only use technology, but, in many cases, use it as their sole method of communicating. Advances in ergonomic technology, which started, in many cases, as accessibility technology, benefit the population at large by keeping people healthy while they work.

Chapter 7 analyzes the free speech clause of the First Amendment and how technology led Congress to develop new standards for applying the First Amendment to new media. This chapter also discusses past attempts at Internet censorship and the Supreme Court's decision to strike down most efforts at censorship.

Computers and the Internet have stretched the boundaries of one-to-one, one-to-many, and many-to-one communication beyond all previously foreseen limits. Chapter 8 explores just a few of the ways in which computers and the Internet are updating and expanding the variety of ways in which people can communicate and collaborate, including *instant messaging, crowdsourcing,* and Wikipedia.

The rapid growth and the wide diversity of computer-based communication technologies indicate that computers are still in their infancy as tools for expressing thoughts and for communicating. The continued widespread use of printed books and of sticky notes on computer monitors provides a hint that computers, for all of their technological sophistication, have still not captured all of the nuances of more traditional forms of communication. Recent advances in e-book readers, smartphones, and speech recognition, however, indicate that developers of communication technology may finally be grasping how to mold such technology to the needs of human users and not the other way around.

1

HISTORY OF ELECTRONIC COMMUNICATION: FROM MORSE CODE TO TALKING THROUGH YOUR COMPUTER

Anthropologists believe that humans first began speaking with each other about 200,000 years ago. The first human writing emerged about 6,000 years ago, in the form of Sumerian *cuneiform* written on clay tablets. It was not until about 170 years ago that humans first became capable of communicating using purely electronic means, when Samuel Morse invented the electronic telegraph. This means that all of the forms of electronic communication in human history—beginning with the telegraph and including the telephone, radio, fax, and the Internet—have been invented and refined in a span of time that is less than 0.1 percent of the history of human communication. This chapter explores this unprecedented burst of innovation by tracing the history of the primary forms of electronic communication technology developed in the last two centuries.

TELEGRAPH

The term *telegraph* refers to various machines used in the 19th and early 20th centuries to send messages to faraway places. Before the telegraph was invented, communicating with someone just a few towns away could take days. The slowness of communication often meant that the outcome of a battle in a far-off land remained unknown for months. Although messages sent by sight and sound, such as with bells or fire, could reach their

1

destinations quickly, such methods were slow, not very reliable, and could only transmit limited amounts of information.

In the years preceding the telegraph's invention, scientists suspected that electricity could be used to communicate detailed messages over long distances. In 1746, the French scientist and abbot Jean-Antoine Nollet (1700–70) conducted an experiment to discover how far and quickly electricity could transmit information along wires. He had 200 monks stand in a line, holding 25-foot (7.6-m) lengths of iron wire connected in series. Nollet connected an electrical battery to the beginning of the wire chain, thereby causing an electrical current to travel down the chain. Each one of the monks received an electrical shock in a period of time that was so short that Nollet could not measure it, thereby demonstrating that electricity could travel over a great distance nearly instantaneously. Experiments such as this, in which electricity was transmitted along wires, were the first step in discovering a way to create an electrical signaling system.

The first telegraph was an optical communication system designed in 1791 by a French inventor named Claude Chappe (1763–1805). Known as the Synchronized System, Chappe's invention consisted of two modified clocks, each of which contained only 10 (rather than 12) numbers and a second hand that moved around the clock face two times per minute. Each of the clocks needed to be synchronized with the other precisely, so that the second hands of both clocks moved at exactly the same speed and passed the same numbers at the same times. Chappe and his brother René were able to send messages to each other using the synchronized clocks while standing a few yards apart. To send a message to René, Claude would use a codebook to translate the message from letters into numbers. Imagine that *Hello* was translated into 8 5 1 2 1 2 1 5 1 5. The first number in this sequence is 8. Claude would transmit this number by waiting until the second hand of his clock passed over the number 8 and then immediately hitting a casserole dish to make a *clang* sound. René would listen for the *clang,* and, upon hearing it, look at his clock to see which number was underneath the second hand. In this example, the number 8 would be underneath the second hand on René's clock because his clock was synchronized with Claude's. René would write down the number 8, and then listen for the next number. By following this process, René would eventually write down the sequence transmitted by Claude: 8 5 1 2 1 2 1 5 1 5. René could then use the codebook to translate this sequence of numbers back into the original message, *Hello.* This method relied for its success not only on the synchronization of the two clocks, but also on the ability of sound to travel quickly over short distances.

Chappe improved his initial system by creating a five-foot-tall (1.5-m) pivoting wooden panel painted black on one side and white on the other. In this system, Chappe could transmit messages by flipping the panel over when the desired number was passed by the second hand on his clock. The recipient of the message used a telescope to view the sender's panel because it was so far away and then referred to a synchronized clock and codebook to translate the numeric message back into letters. Chappe tested his new system by sending a message to someone located 10 miles (16 km) away. It took four minutes to use this system to send the phrase "If you succeed, you will soon bask in glory." Chappe named his invention télégraphe, meaning "far writer."

Chappe created yet another optical message transmission system in 1793. It included two rotating arms called indicators that were attached to a rotating bar called a regulator. The regulator was capable of rotating horizontally or vertically while the arms could rotate in one of seven different positions in 45-degree increments. The telegraph was positioned on the roof of a tower and the operator inside controlled the arms of the telegraph. The operator sent a message by moving each arm into a position that corresponded with a different letter, number, or common syllable in the codebook. Because telegraph towers were positioned in a long line with each tower stationed a few miles from the next, it was necessary for operators to use a telescope to view telegraph messages. The receiving operator used a codebook containing 92 codes that represented numbers, letters, and syllables to translate the message into words. A total of 8,464 words and phrases could be represented using the code.

In 1809, Samuel Soemmering (1755–1830) created an electrochemical telegraph, meaning that it transmitted messages using a combination of electrical signals and chemical reactions. Soemmering's telegraph system required the placement of 26 wires with gold electrodes in acid. At one end, each of the 26 wires that represented a letter in the German alphabet was connected to both a sending terminal and a receiving terminal. A recipient was able to interpret the message by the bubbles coming from the wires that were labeled with each letter of the alphabet. It was only possible to send one letter at a time. One benefit of this system was that it did not rely on the senses of the human operators, in the way that Chappe's telegraphs relied on the recipient's ability to hear or see the coded message sent by the message's sender. Soemmering's system was therefore not only capable of sending messages over longer distances than Chappe's, but was also more reliable because human hearing and vision have limited accuracy.

The use of electric current in telegraphs such as Soemmering's was a significant step toward the creation of a telegraph system that transmitted messages solely using electrical signals. The British inventor William Sturgeon (1793–1850) took a further step in this direction in 1825 when he demonstrated the first electromagnet, using electric current to cause a seven-ounce (198-g) piece of iron wrapped in wires to lift a nine-pound (4-kg) weight. In 1830, the American-born scientist Joseph Henry (1797–1878) discovered that electric current sent by wire for more than a mile could activate an electromagnet, thereby causing a bell to strike.

Building on these and other advances, Samuel Morse (1791–1872) invented the first purely electrical telegraph capable of sending messages encoded in electrical signals through wires over very long distances. Morse, a professor of art and design at New York University, had become committed to creating an electrical telegraph system after hearing the story about Nollet's experiment while on a ship traveling from Europe to the United States in 1832.

In 1835, Morse successfully transmitted electrical signals along wires using pulses of electric current, which caused a marker to write code on a piece of paper. One year later, Morse revised the method to print dots (·) and dashes (–). To transmit a message with a telegraph key, a hand-operated device for sending *Morse code,* a telegraph operator pressed the knob on the machine. To transmit a dot, the operator pressed down on the knob and released it quickly, while to transmit a dash the operator held down the knob for a longer time. For example, the operator sent the message *Hello* using the following dot and dash sequence:

$$\cdots\cdot \;\; \cdot \;\; \cdot\text{--}\cdot\cdot \;\; \cdot\text{--}\cdot\cdot \;\; \text{---}\cdot$$

If the message to be transmitted contained more than one word, the operator indicated a space between words by releasing the knob to the off position for a time equivalent to a medium gap, represented by 0000000, or seven units of word spacing. When a telegraph station received the message, the receiver's telegraph made a clicking noise as it printed the dots and dashes on a piece of paper.

Morse Code

A	.-	N	-.	0	-----	
B	-...	O	---	1	.----	
C	-.-.	P	.--.	2	..---	
D	-..	Q	--.-	3	...--	
E	.	R	.-.	4	....-	
F	..-.	S	...	5	.....	
G	--.	T	-	6	-....	
H	....	U	..-	7	--...	
I	..	V	...-	8	---..	
J	.---	W	.--	9	----.	
K	-.-	X	-..-	Fullstop	.-.-.-	
L	.-..	Y	-.--	Comma	--..--	
M	--	Z	--..	Query	..--..	

© Infobase Learning

Morse code is a set of symbols that are used to transmit and receive messages, known as telegrams, using telegraph machines. Morse code includes symbols for letters, numbers, and punctuation marks. Each symbol may contain one or more dots, one or more dashes, or a combination of dots and dashes. A dot is transmitted as a short electrical pulse, while a dash is transmitted as a longer electrical pulse (typically three times as long as a dot). A telegraph operator typically generates dots and dashes by pressing down a paddle for shorter and longer periods of time, respectively, to generate electrical signals corresponding to the characters in the message to be transmitted. The telegraph was the primary form of high-speed electrical communication until the invention of the telephone. Morse code remains in use today in fields such as aviation and amateur radio.

The operator translated the dots and dashes into letters by using a codebook to decipher the message. Operators were later able to translate the clicking noise into dots and dashes without the use of paper.

In 1842, Morse demonstrated the ability of the telegraph to send messages by placing wires between two rooms in the U.S. Capitol. Based on this success, Congress allocated $30,000 toward building an experimental telegraph line.

Upon its completion, on May 24, 1844, Morse sent the message, "What hath God wrought," from the Supreme Court in Washington to Baltimore, Maryland, about 40 miles (64.4 km) away.

Morse code made communication over long distances much easier and faster than it had ever been before. Soon telegraph lines throughout the United States connected towns and cities. In 1851, England was connected to other European countries by undersea cable, and in 1866 a cable laid on the bottom of the Atlantic Ocean connected the United States to England. The telegraph was eventually used to standardize time, transmit news, and send messages in real time to others. Because the telegraph was capable of delivering news nearly instantly, many believed that it would replace newspapers. Analysts predicted that newspapers would move from reporting the news to providing commentary and analysis on the news. Unlike printed newspapers, however, the telegraph proved unable to deliver news to a large number of people. Newspaper publishers found a way to use the telegraph's news reporting capability to increase sales. As breaking news occurred, newspapers published the story in installments. For example, one story with three developments would result in the publication of three editions that day. The telegraph, consequently, led to long-term changes in the way news was reported. Today's news organization still report news as it occurs, but use the instantaneous delivery systems of television and the Internet to report updates nearly instantaneously.

The way companies conducted business also changed as a result of the telegraph. Before the telegraph, messages sent from New York to Chicago typically arrived after a monthlong journey. Often, messages were outdated by the time of arrival. The telegraph changed business relationships and the receipt of information because of its ability to provide almost immediate communication. Through the telegraph, for instance, a business became aware of the receipt of a shipment within weeks rather than waiting months to learn the result. It also became possible to conduct business at any time. This was especially relevant in business transactions between companies in the United States and companies overseas. Consequently, businessmen no longer retired undisturbed to the comfort of their homes after a day at the office. Instead, a telegram from a business in another country might arrive with a purchase order request at any time of day or night. If such a telegram arrived in the evening, the businessman would leave his family at home to return to the office to place the order. Consequently, the telegraph created immediate access to other businesses as well as the possibility of immediate responses.

The company Western Union came to dominate the telegraph industry. In 1867, 5.8 million messages were sent across its telegraph lines. By 1900, this number increased to 63.2 million. Its market share of 90 percent in every state was a concern not only to its rivals, Pacific Telegraph Company and Postal Telegraph Company, but also received the attention of members of Congress. Although bills were introduced in Congress calling for regulation of the telegraph industry, such efforts ultimately failed due to Western Union's powerful lobby. Nevertheless, telegraph usage would decline in the 20th century as people increasingly turned to the telephone for long-distance communication.

TELEPHONE

Although the telegraph improved long-distance communication, it did have disadvantages. For example, it was too expensive for the average person, trained operators were required to transmit and receive messages, and messages were sent in written code rather than by human voice. Alexander Graham Bell (1847–1922), a professor of vocal physiology and elocution at Boston University, believed that the telegraph system could be improved by creating a telegraph that could send multiple messages at once. While theorizing about such a "multiple telegraph" in 1874, Bell developed the theory of the telephone. Bell had been experimenting with a *phonautograph,* a machine used to assist the deaf in improving their speech. As a deaf person spoke, a membrane in the phonautograph would vibrate in response to the speech. A reed attached to the membrane recorded the vibrations by drawing a pattern on a piece of glass coated in charcoal. The deaf speaker could then compare the drawing of his or her own speech with drawings representing patterns of correct speech in an attempt to improve at speaking. Bell theorized that if it was possible to transform speech into an electrical current that could vibrate the reed of the phonautograph, then it was possible to send speech using electrical signals alone over a wire.

Bell soon thereafter invented such a device, and on March 7, 1876, he received a patent for it, entitled, "Improvements in Telegraphy." Elisha Gray, an electrician, had also filed a patent application for a "speaking telephone" just a few hours after Bell's application. Bell, however, was granted the patent because he filed the application first. Nevertheless, a legal battle over the patent ensued, with Bell eventually prevailing. Three days after receiving the patent, Bell made his first telephone call to his assistant, Thomas Watson (1854–1934). The first words heard on Bell's machine were "Mr. Watson, come here, I want to see you!" The initial machine was only one-way, but Bell later invented a two-way version, enabling Watson and Bell to hold their first two-way telephone conversation in October 1876.

Bell's telephone was comprised of a thin metal sheet that covered the end of a tube. A metal needle was attached to the sheet and sat dipped in a cup of acid. The depth that the needle was dipped into the acid was determined by the strength of the electric current. When someone spoke into the tube, the metal sheet vibrated in response, which in turn caused the needle to vibrate. The changing vibration of the needle within the acid caused the electric current transmitted by the telephone to change in time to match the speaker's voice. At the other end of the telephone wire, a coil of wire wrapped around a piece of wire received the vibrating electric current, thereby creating an electromagnet. The variances in the electric current changed the force of the electromagnet, which made the metal sheet vibrate and thereby create sound.

Telephones enabled people to communicate much more quickly than by using the telegraph. To transmit the message "Hello, how are you doing?" by telegraph would take nearly four minutes, even with trained telegraph operators. An untrained person could transmit the same message by telephone in fewer than five seconds. This was a significant improvement in the speed of communication. Additionally, it was much easier to communicate by telephone because telephone communication made it unnecessary to translate a code into words. Instead, the user could simply speak into the receiver of the phone and listen for a response in the earpiece. Speaking by telephone was similar to speaking in person.

Telephones were first operated over existing telegraph lines, thereby enabling telephones to be brought into use relatively quickly and inexpensively, without the need to build new transmission lines. Due to the high cost of telephone

(opposite page) Alexander Graham Bell, the inventor of the telephone, engages in the first telephone communication from New York to Chicago as a crowd looks on. *(North Wind Picture Archives/Alamy)*

equipment, the earliest telephone customers leased, rather than purchased, their telephones. In order to speak to someone by phone, it was necessary for a wire to directly connect the phones. For instance, one telephone was often installed at a person's home, while the other telephone was installed at the person's office. Each phone was connected to the other by a direct line. To communicate in multiple locations it was necessary to buy a phone for each location and to have all of them connected directly to each other by wire.

As the number of telephones in use grew, it became increasingly expensive to connect so many telephones to each other directly. As a result, all lines were eventually connected to a central switchboard. When someone wanted to make a call (the caller), he would pick up his telephone handset, which would connect him to a human operator located at the switchboard. The caller would tell the switchboard operator the name of the person he wished to call (the callee). In response, the operator connected a cable on the switchboard between a plug connected to the caller's phone and a plug connected to the callee's phone, thereby completing a circuit between the two phones. The switchboard operator would hang up and the caller could then speak directly to the callee. These early calls were made from telephones that required the use of an earpiece paired with a mouthpiece. While holding the earpiece up to the ear, the user spoke into the cone-shaped mouthpiece. At this time, it was not possible to make long-distance calls. Instead, callers could only call people having phones within the same local area, connected to the same physical switchboard.

Phone calls can be made today without the use of human switchboard operators because computerized switches now connect telephone callers to callees automatically. Every telephone is linked through a network of exchanges and radio links. Tone dialing, which is performed by pressing the numbers on the keypad, was made possible by the computerization of *switches*. The computer is able to connect a call by recognizing the unique sound that each key creates. Each row and column has a unique tone. Each key, therefore, creates a unique combination of tones that represents its row and column.

The mobile telephone was conceived in 1947 but not created until 1978. Unlike landline telephone connections established through wires, a cellular phone contains a radio transmitter and receiver that provide a link to other phones by radio waves. Cellular phones work in an area called a cell. Every cell has a base station with a different frequency. When a cellular phone is used, a base station receives a signal. As the cellular user moves into another cell, another base station in the surrounding area receives the signals. The base station then sends signals to the central exchange for the cellular phone to switch to the new radio frequency. Communication through cellular phones allows people to communicate from anywhere that a connection is available.

FACSIMILE

The *facsimile* (fax) machine is a mechanism used to transmit printed information over a telephone line to another location. In 1843, the Scottish mechanic Alexander Bain (1818–1903) invented the first fax machine. Bain's machine leveraged technology he had previously invented for use in an electric clock and chemical telegraph. Bain's fax machine used a stylus, which functioned as a swinging pendulum to produce electrical pulses as it swung over the raised image on a metal plate. The stylus moved over the entire length of the image, and the receiving device, which also had a pendulum, received the electric pulses through an electric wire. As the sending device transmitted electric pulses, special electrically sensitive paper at the receiving end printed the image. Although Bain received a British patent for his fax machine, the device was not sufficiently reliable to be manufactured and sold as a commercial product.

Other inventors continued to improve upon Bain's device during the 1900s. In 1914, Édouard Belin (1876–1963) invented the Belinograph, which closely resembled the modern fax machine. The machine used a strong beam of light generated by a photoelectric cell to scan an image placed on a rotating drum. The machine converted light, or the absence of light, into electrical pulses that were then used to transmit the image across a wire. The American Telephone and Telegraph Company (AT&T) made further advancements in fax technology with its creation of the telephotography machine in 1924. The machine successfully sent pictures from political conventions in Cleveland, Ohio, and Chicago, Illinois, to newspapers in New York City. Two years later, RCA created the radio-photo, a fax machine that transmitted data over the air using radio broadcasting technology. The first radio fax transmission sent across the North American continent occurred on March 4, 1955.

Xerox made a significant advancement in fax technology in 1964. The Long Distance Xerography (LDX) device was the first fax machine capable of high-speed transmission. Two years later, Xerox joined with the Magnavox Company to create the Magnafax Telecopier, a device that could send and receive documents over a standard telephone line. Although the telecopier required six minutes to transmit a single letter-sized page, it nonetheless represented a significant improvement over previous fax technology, which required the installation of separate transmission lines dedicated specifically to sending and receiving faxes.

Nevertheless, because these early fax machines were expensive and difficult to use, they were relatively unpopular. The introduction in 1988 of fax machines capable of transmitting documents at 9,600 bits per second led to tremendous growth in the use of fax machines. A standard protocol for fax transmission, known as the Group 3 protocol, was adopted by the communications industry in 1983. As a result, many businesses began using fax machines instead of postal mail for regular correspondence, and individuals began using fax machines for transmitting personal correspondence in significantly larger numbers. The introduction of low-cost fax machines and all-in-one machines that combined the capabilities of printers, scanners, and fax machines led to further growth in fax usage.

Modern fax machines use a photo sensor instead of a rotating drum to transmit an image of a document. To use such machines to transmit a document, the document is placed facedown on a glass plate, under which the photo sensor is positioned. The user dials the phone number for the receiving fax machine by using a touch-tone keypad on the fax machine. The user then presses a key such as fax/send to initiate transmission of the document to the receiving fax machine. The sensor in the sending machine moves underneath the document and digitizes the document by dividing it into a grid of dots. A single bit, which may have a value of either 0 or 1, represents each dot. Each dark area in the document is converted into a bit having a value of 1, whereas each light area is converted into a bit having a value of 0. The result of this conversion process is a grid of bits, each representing a very small area of the document (often a square that is 1/150th of an inch on each side). This grid is referred to as a *bitmap*. The entire bitmap is transmitted by the sending fax machine to the receiving fax machine as a sequence of bits (0s and 1s). The receiving fax machine receives the bit sequences and translates the 0s and 1s back into a two-dimensional grid of dots, thereby recreating the original document image. With the creation of new technology, users are able to send and receive faxes using computers and cell phones and to convert faxes into *e-mail* messages and vice versa. Although many observers of technology predicted the death of fax technology in the 1990s in response to the growth of e-mail, the Web, and other more sophisticated forms of electronic communication, faxes have remained a mainstay of personal and business communication precisely because of their simplicity.

RADIO

Many forms of modern electronic communication technology use electromagnetic waves to transmit information because these waves can travel through space over long distances, whether or not the space contains air. These properties of electromagnetic waves give them an advantage over sound waves, which require air or some other medium through which to travel, and traditional (noncellular) telephone communications, which require wires. Furthermore, most kinds of electromagnetic waves are not visible to the human eye or audible to the human ear. As a result, they can travel around—and even through—human bodies, buildings, and other spaces occupied by people without creating distractions.

Every signal transmitted using electromagnetic waves has a particular frequency. Light visible to the human eye is an example of an electromagnetic wave. Different frequencies of visible light are perceived by the human eye as different colors, ranging from red (with frequencies ranging from ~480–405 Terahertz) to violet (with frequencies ranging from ~785–665 Terahertz), with all the colors of the rainbow in between. In fact, the acronym ROYGBIV, pronounced like "Roy G. Biv," is used as a mnemonic to remember the range of colors in the visible light spectrum: Red, Orange, Yellow, Green, Blue, Indigo, and Violet.

The spectrum (range of frequencies) of light visible to humans occupies only a very small portion of the total electromagnetic radiation spectrum. Examples of electromagnetic radiation that is not visible to the human eye include radio waves, microwaves, infrared radiation, ultraviolet radiation, X-rays, and gamma rays.

Radio waves, which have a wavelength that is about a million times longer than that of visible light, were the first kind of nonvisible electromagnetic radiation harnessed by humans to transmit messages. Because radio waves are invisible, it was not until the Scottish physicist James Clerk Maxwell (1831–79) predicted that they existed in the 1860s that scientists began to explore the possibility of transmitting information using radio waves. The German scientist Heinrich Hertz (1857–94) proved the existence of radio waves in 1866 when he demonstrated that rapid variations of electric current could be used to create a wave that was similar to a light or heat wave.

Two inventors, Nikola Tesla (1856–1943) of Serbia and Guglielmo Marconi (1874–1937) of Italy, made significant advances in radio technology just before the end of the 19th century. In 1891, Tesla devised a method to produce radio signals at various frequencies and then to transmit them over a distance. Tragically, Tesla's lab was destroyed by fire before he could complete his work. Drawing on the developments of Tesla, Marconi used radio waves to send a wireless message that traveled 1.24 miles (2 km) in Italy in 1896. Marconi named his development the *radiotelegraph* because, like traditional telegraphs, it transmitted messages using Morse code, but unlike traditional telegraphs it transmitted such messages without wires. Marconi's continued experimentation led to the first confirmed transatlantic radio communication in 1902.

The radiotelegraph used Morse's dot- and dash-based code system, encoded as short sounds called bleeps, to send messages using transmitters called spark-gap machines. Long and short bleep sounds were made by switching the radio signal to the off and on position for different durations of time. In 1901, the U.S. Navy was the first to use the radiotelegraph to communicate between ships, to communicate between ships and the shore, and to transmit rescue messages from people stranded at sea. The distress signal *SOS* originated as a radiotelegraph signal consisting of the letters *S, O,* and *S* transmitted repeatedly in Morse code. (Interestingly, although SOS often is believed to stand for "save our ship," it was chosen originally simply because the sequence S-O-S was easy to remember in Morse code.) The radiotelegraph proved much more efficient and reliable for such communications than visual signals or homing pigeons.

Improvements to radio transmitters eventually led to radio transmission of the human voice. In 1907, the American inventor Lee De Forest (1873–1961) designed the *audion,* a device that used a three-electrode vacuum tube to enhance the receipt of radio waves. This and a variety of other innovations made it possible to transmit not only Morse code but also the human voice. The American inventor Reginald Aubrey Fessenden (1866–1932) typically is credited with producing the first radio transmission of the human voice over a distance of about one mile (1.6 km) in December 1900. Although the quality of the transmission was too low to make it useful commercially, it did prove in theory that human speech and other sounds could be transmitted using radio waves.

The earliest radio transmitters transmitted signals that occupied the entire radio spectrum. As a result, it was not possible for more than one radio signal to be transmitted at a time without interfering with others and making it impossible for any of the signals to be received and deciphered by transmitters. This problem was solved with the invention of *amplitude modulated (AM) radio* by Fessenden and De Forest. Amplitude modulation refers to the fact that AM radio transmits sound by varying the amplitude of the transmitted electrical signal over time to reflect variations in the sound being transmitted over time. The receiver detects these variations in amplitude of the radio signal and converts them back into variations in sound, thereby enabling the original sound to be reconstructed and played back by the receiver.

It was not until 1916 that the first sustained radio broadcast occurred, when Harold Power, through his radio company American Radio and Research Company (AMRAD), transmitted a three-hour radio broadcast from Tufts University. Four years later, Westinghouse's radio station KDKA-Pittsburgh broadcast the results of the presidential election between Warren G. Harding and James M. Cox. Thereafter, KDKA and numerous other radio stations began broadcasting news, dance bands, and other regular programs. The radio soon became the primary form of entertainment for many families.

Radio technology continued to develop throughout the early 20th century. In 1933, Edwin Howard Armstrong (1890–1954) invented *frequency modulated (FM) radio.* Frequency modulation refers to the fact that FM radio transmits sound by varying the frequency of the transmitted electrical signal over time to reflect variations in the sound being transmitted over time. The primary benefit of FM radio is that FM signals are less susceptible to being disrupted by noise and interference. As a result, FM radio signals generally are more suitable for transmitting music and other audio requiring high-quality reception and playback than AM radio can provide. This is why most AM radio stations today transmit news and talk shows, while most music is transmitted on FM radio stations.

Radio waves can be used to perform functions other than transmitting speech and other kinds of sound. For example, *radar* systems use radio waves to track planes and other airborne objects that are not visible to the human eye. To track such objects, a radar system transmits radio waves in all directions. Waves that strike a plane or other object bounce off the object and are received by the radar system, which uses the direction and timing of receipt to calculate the direction and distance of the object from the radar transmitter.

Satellite radio, which has seen significant growth in recent years, uses satellites orbiting the Earth to transmit analog or digital radio signals. Many of the same news, music, and entertainment programs that are transmitted using traditional terrestrial radio transmitters are now also transmitted by satellite. Furthermore, many additional stations are available only by satellite. One benefit of satellite radio is that many satellite radio stations are available across an entire country or continent. On the other hand, satellite radio systems typically are only available for a fee and require the receiver to have a clear line of sight to the satellites in order to receive the signal.

Similarly, *Internet radio* provides yet another way to listen to radio stations. It is now possible to use a standard Web browser or media player software (such as Windows Media Player or RealPlayer) to listen to any of thousands of radio stations over the Internet, including both Internet versions of traditional radio stations and Internet-only stations. This makes it possible for radio listeners to listen to radio stations using any device with an Internet connection and speakers or a headphone jack, such as a desktop computer, laptop computer, cellular telephone, or digital music player (such as an Apple iPod).

For example, Pandora allows users to create personalized Internet radio stations based on their preferences. LastFM keeps a record of what music its users listen to and then recommends similar music and concerts to listen to and attend. Rhapsody is a popular service that gives its subscribers access to unlimited streaming music for a flat monthly fee, eliminating the need to purchase individual songs. New services with additional features and pricing schemes are being released all the time.

TELEVISION

Success at using radio waves to transmit sound led scientists to explore ways to use radio waves and other kinds of electromagnetic waves to transmit pictures, eventually leading to the invention of television. Early experiments at achieving this goal tended to focus on the creation of two types of television systems—mechanical televisions and electronic televisions. One of the first successes resulted from an 1873 experiment by Willoughby Smith (1828–91) with selenium and light, which led to the discovery of how to transform images into electronic signals. Smith's discovery helped Paul Nipkow (1860–1940), an engineering student working on the creation of a mechanical television, to create a disk camera called a Nipkow Disk in 1884. This rotating disk camera analyzed pictures by rapidly rotating a disk positioned between a picture and a selenium element that was sensitive to light. The image projected by this system had only 18 lines of resolution, compared to the 200 lines of resolution on modern analog televisions and as many as 1,080 lines of resolution on modern high-definition televisions.

While progress continued with the creation of a mechanical television, other inventors were working to create an electronic television. The 1897 invention of the cathode-ray tube (CRT), also known as the picture tube, spurred the invention of the electronic television. A cathode-ray tube displays images by firing an electron beam at a the back surface of the television screen, which is coated with a phosphorescent material. The electrons cause the phosphors to emit light in a pattern that represents the transmitted image. The electron beam scans across the entire screen very quickly, one row at a time, to create a single frame of video, which is displayed for a very short time (often 1/60th of a second) before creating the next image. Therefore, although a television broadcast consists of a sequence of still images, such appears to represent movement in much the way that hand-drawn cartoons appear animated when their individual frames are displayed quickly in sequence.

In 1907, geometric patterns were transmitted over the air and displayed on a screen for the first time using a CRT. In 1927, Philo Farnsworth (1906–71) built the image dissector, an electronic television system that transmitted an image of a dollar by the technique of scanning the image with a beam of electrons. This was the first functional television capable of projecting an image with 60 horizontal lines. One year later, the first U.S. television station—W3XK in Washington, D.C.—was licensed for business. Building on the Nipkow Disk, John Baird (1888–1946) of England created the first working mechanical television when he televised pictures of moving objects in 1924, a human face in 1925, and a moving object in 1926.

Although the first television screens were small, the first televisions as a whole were bulky because they contained very large CRTs. As picture tubes became smaller, so did television sets. Early televisions did not have remote controls. Instead, viewers adjusted the volume and changed channels by turning a knob on the television set. Typically, fewer than 15 channels were available in most cities. Televisions also had antennas, known as rabbit ears because of their shape, which allowed the set to receive the signals that were broadcast by a larger antenna at a television station. Furthermore, for more two decades after televisions became available commercially, they could only display images in black and white.

Even though the television first became available in the 1920s, most people continued to listen to the radio. By 1936, only 200 television sets were in use worldwide. In 1939, the World's Fair in New York City provided many people with their first glimpse of television, in the form of 13 black-and-white televisions the size of toasters on display. Visitors at the opening day of the fair witnessed a broadcast by President Franklin D. Roosevelt, in which he became the first American president to appear on television. Fair visitors also had the opportunity to watch baseball games and other types of entertainment such as puppet shows on television. Television amazed viewers, but most could not afford to buy one until after World War II. A television set in 1940 cost between $200 and $1,000—as much as $15,000 in today's dollars. For purposes of comparison, a new car cost about $1,000 in 1940. By the 1950s, television sets became more commonplace in American homes as prices decreased significantly.

It was not until 1953 that the first television sets that were capable of displaying color broadcasts became available. Although the first patents for color television sets were granted in 1904 for a mechanical system and again in 1925 for an electronic system, such televisions remained too expensive and complex to be sold as consumer products for almost a half-century.

Just like radio broadcasting, broadcast television programs were originally transmitted using radio waves, although at higher frequencies than radio programs. Although at first all television programs were transmitted using ground-based transmitters, they are now also transmitted using satellites and through cables directly into people's homes.

Just as radio stations have begun to make their programs available over the Internet, so too have television stations and networks begun to migrate to the

(continues on page 22)

10011101001010101001100101110110101001010 01

Interactivity

The technological developments made over the last few hundred years have enabled various kinds of interactivity. Before these advancements, people could engage in one-to-one communication—in which exactly one person communicated with exactly one other person—either in person or by letter. In-person communication, of course, was limited by the presence of the other person. Communicating by letter or sending a message through a messenger required waiting for a response. Delivery of a message was only as fast as the messenger could travel, and it was not even possible to send a letter in the United States until 1775. The introduction of the telegraph revolutionized long-distance communication by giving people the ability to send messages quickly and over long distances with relative ease. Communication by telegraph, however, required skilled telegraph operators to translate the message at both ends. The introduction of the telephone gave people a way to communicate directly and instantaneously, regardless of distance and without intermediaries. Modern technologies such as e-mail and text messaging provide additional ways to communicate one-to-one.

Various forms of one-to-many communication, in which one person communicates with many people, have also existed for almost as long as communication has existed. The town crier could use his booming voice to announce important news to an entire town simultaneously. A smoke signal can be viewed by many people over a wide distance. Newspapers are written by a small team of people but read by thousands. While newspapers initially provided the primary way of communicating news, advertisements, and other information, the introduction of the radio and television offered additional ways to reach more people through the transmission of the human voice through the radio and sound and moving images through a television set.

Advancements in computer technology have facilitated one-to-many communication in a variety of ways. For example, both individuals and companies use e-mail for mass communication, eliminating the need to send separate messages to each recipient. It is common for companies to create a distribution list containing the e-mail addresses of all of their customers and to send a single

(continues)

100111010010101010011001011101101010010 01

(continued)

e-mail message to everyone on the list simultaneously, thereby achieving the same effect as an old-fashioned newsletter or flyer much more quickly and inexpensively. Unlike traditional mailings, however, e-mails can be customized for each recipient, such as by including the recipient's name and providing customized offers based on the recipient's past buying history and preferences. Web-based *chat rooms* also allow one-to-many communication. Online chat, which is typically text based, is used to communicate messages in real time to others in the same chat room. In this forum, one person is able to post messages for receipt by multiple people.

Many-to-many communication allows conversational exchange between many individuals. Because today's technology allows people to receive and contribute information in ways that do not require physical presence, several types of communication methods are available. A conference call, which is a telephone call that connects multiple people, is a forum for a group meeting over the telephone. Typically, a participant calls a special number and enters a personalized code to access the conference call. E-mail is also a convenient method for many-to-many communication. Other Internet-based methods of many-to-many communication include videoconferencing, chat room conferences, and the use of collaboration software designed to create a cooperative work system for authoring joint documents and completing group projects. Such software enables changes made by one person to be made visible to all other members of the group instantaneously.

One of the most popular forums for communication with others is social networking Web sites. The purpose of these sites is to enable people to stay connected with their existing friends and family and to meet new people. The most prominent site, Facebook, allows a quick and easy way to share information with multiple people through a subscriber's personal page. Every subscriber creates a personal profile that includes information about the subscriber, such as the subscriber's interests, relationship status, photographs, and video footage. Facebook subscribers, for instance, can also meet new friends by joining networks organized by region, workplace, and school, or join a group organized by common interest. Users on such sites can communicate with many people or just one individual through instant messaging, internal e-mail, comments, blogs, and chat.

Twitter, the popular social networking and microblogging service, has proven both useful for enabling friends and family to stay in touch and influential in newsworthy events such as the uprising in Egypt and the conflict in Libya. Iran operated one of the world's most sophisticated Web-filtering systems in response to street protests following the 2009 presidential election, shutting down all text messaging. Losing their prime communications tool led protestors to turn to Twitter and old-fashioned word of mouth, creating a loose worldwide network of sympathizers that rose up to keep activists connected. Similarly, in early 2011, the Egyptian government cut off nearly all access to the Internet and shut down cell phone service. Activists inside and outside the country of 80 million people worked around the shutdown by accessing the Internet using means such as dial-up Internet connections in other countries. They were then able to communicate with overseas friends and relatives using e-mail, Twitter, and other social media.

Communication is either *synchronous* or *asynchronous*. In synchronous communication, both parties are engaged in a conversation at the same time and respond to each other immediately, much like a face-to-face discussion or a telephone conversation. Even one-way communications can be synchronous. For example, a television broadcast is synchronous because the viewer watches the broadcast at the same time as it is received by the viewer's television. Asynchronous communication, in contrast, refers to time-delayed communication. Communication by written letter and e-mail are two examples of asynchronous communication, because in both cases some time passes between when a message is sent and the time at which it is retrieved by the recipient. The recipient may not read and/or respond to the message until minutes, hours, or days after it was received. In practice, however, sometimes e-mail communication can be synchronous if both parties immediately read and respond to each other's e-mail messages. Similarly, even a synchronous form of communication such as a television broadcast can become asynchronous if the viewer records a television program and then watches the recording at a later date. As these examples illustrate, whether a particular message is synchronous or asynchronous depends not only on the kind of technology that is used to transmit it, but also on how that technology is used in a particular situation.

(continued from page 18)

Internet. Internet television lagged behind Internet radio just as traditional television lagged behind traditional radio, due to the complexities introduced by the need to transmit and display images in connection with television programs. In recent years, however, Internet television has become more widespread as home computers have increased in power, and as high-speed, always-on Internet connections have become more commonplace and less expensive. It is now possible to watch many broadcast television programs online lawfully and free using services such as Hulu (although there are also numerous Web sites that illegally host copyrighted content). Other services, such as iTunes, offer certain television programs for purchase or rent for a small fee. Companies such as Netflix and Amazon now make many television programs available for purchase and rent not only through computers but also through digital video recorders so that such programs may be viewed directly on the television, eliminating the need for a separate computer.

COMPUTER COMMUNICATIONS

Computers can communicate with each other using a wide variety of intermediate devices, such as *modems, routers,* and *switches.* In the early days of computing, one of the most effective ways to connect two computers for purposes of transferring information between them was to directly connect using a *serial cable* or a *parallel cable.* A serial cable transmits digital data one bit at a time, much like cars exiting a highway must converge from several lanes into a single lane on the exit ramp. As a result, serial communication is relatively slow but simple and inexpensive to implement. A parallel cable can transmit multiple bits of information (such as 8, 16, 32, or 64 bits) simultaneously (in parallel), thereby achieving faster rates of transmission but requiring larger, heavier, more expensive cables. Once two computers are directly connected by a serial or parallel cable, each computer can transmit information directly to the other computer over the cable.

Although serial communication is slow relative to parallel communication, serial transmission can still be fast enough for many purposes. For example, *Universal Serial Bus (USB)* cables are serial cables that are widely used today to transmit data between computers and their attached mice, keyboards, printers, and hard disk drives without any noticeable delay for most purposes.

Regardless of the particular type of cable that is used, the primary benefit of communicating using a direct cable connection is that it is simple and inexpensive to set up and operate. No special network hardware or software is required. The primary disadvantage of a direct cable connection, however, is that it cannot easily be used to connect more than two computers and it can only be used to transmit information over very small distances (usually a few feet). Therefore, direct cable connections are not useful for most forms of computer networking today.

A more advanced kind of networking device is the modem. Modem is a combination of the terms *modulator* and *demodulator,* because to transmit data from one computer to another using modems involves: (1) using a first modem

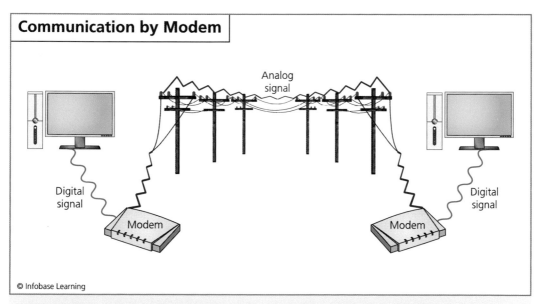

Communication by Modem

© Infobase Learning

Although computers process and transmit data in digital form, until recently all telephone communications were transmitted using analog signals. As a result, for one computer to transmit a message to another computer over analog telephone lines, each computer would need to be connected to its own modem. The first computer would generate a digital signal. The first computer's modem would then convert the digital signal into an analog signal and transmit the analog signal over the analog telephone lines. The analog signal would then be received by the second computer's modem, which would convert the analog signal back into digital form and provide the reconstructed digital signal to the second computer. The process of converting signals from digital to analog form and then back again is known as modulation and demodulation. The term *modem* was created by combining the first two letters of modulation with the first three letters of demodulation.

connected to the first computer to modulate (convert) a digital signal from the first computer into an analog signal, which the first computer's modem transmits over an analog telephone line; and (2) using a second modem connected to the second computer to receive the analog signal and demodulate (convert) the analog signal back into the original digital signal. In this way, a modem enables two digital computers to transmit digital data to each other over analog phone lines. This ability of modems to leverage existing analog phone lines as transmission lines for computer communications led to an explosive growth in the design, manufacture, and sale of modems to businesses and consumers in the 1980s and 1990s. Modems made it possible for people to communicate with each other by computer without needing to purchase and install separate transmission lines. By the late 1990s, most home computers that were connected to the Internet did so using modems.

The first mass-produced modems were designed in the 1950s for use in the U.S. Semi-Automatic Ground Environment (SAGE) air defense system. Such modems connected computers at radar stations, air force bases, and other military installations to SAGE centers located throughout the country. The Bell 103 modem, which made its commercial debut in 1962, could transfer data at 300 bits per second. Significant progress would be made, slowly but surely over the next 30 years, to achieve modem technology which, by 1996, could transmit data at 56,000 bits per second over the same standard telephone lines—almost 200 times as fast as the Bell 103. This is a remarkable achievement, given the fact that such telephone lines were originally intended to transmit analog voice signals, not digital data signals. This increase in modem communication speed led to a tremendous growth in Internet use in the late 1990s, because it made viewing of Web sites with graphics feasible without long wait times.

Physical limitations in the communications capabilities of standard telephone lines, however, limited the speed that could be achieved by analog modem technology. Consequently, broadband modems of various kinds were developed to supersede such limitations and have since become a popular alternative. Broadband is a type of transmission technique that is able to carry multiple data channels over one wire. High-speed digital subscriber line (DSL) service, for example, combines voice and data channels on one line, allowing computer users to simultaneously hold telephone conversations and engage in high-speed data transmission over the same telephone line. Cable modems, also a kind of broadband modem technology, allow computers to communicate over the Internet in both directions over cable television networks.

As Internet service providers (ISPs) have continued to upgrade their networks to overcome the limitations of earlier analog telephone lines, home computer users can now use broadband modems to connect to the Internet over high-speed cable and fiber optic connections, enabling Internet connection speeds of as high as 25 megabits per second in the United States—almost 500 times as fast as the 56,000 bits per second modems of the 1990s, and more than 80,000 times as fast as the first Bell 103 modem of the 1960s.

If a computer user has a broadband modem and desires to connect only one computer to the Internet, then she may connect her computer directly to the broadband modem. Connecting multiple computers to the Internet, however, usually requires first connecting a router or switch to the modem, and then connecting the multiple computers to the router or switch. The router or switch usually has several ports, each of which may be connected to a separate computer. Some ISPs provide their customers with cable modems having built-in routers or switches to avoid the need for the customer to purchase and install an additional device. Corporations, universities, government agencies, and other organizations also use routers and switches to enable multiple computers to share the same Internet connection simultaneously. The primary function of a router or switch is to ensure that communications are directed to and from the correct devices. For example, if one of several computers connected to a switch requests to be directed to Amazon.com, then the switch ensures that the site is downloaded to the computer that requested it, rather than to another computer connected to the same switch.

More generally, routers and switches are located throughout the Internet and other networks to ensure that information reaches its intended destination. Returning to the example of a computer that requests to be directed to Amazon, the computer transmits a request for Amazon to the switch to which the computer is directly connected. That switch forwards this request to another switch or router, which uses information in the request to transmit the request to another router or switch that is closer to the Amazon server. Eventually, possibly after passing through many routers and/or switches, the request reaches the Amazon server, which responds to the request by transmitting the requested

(continues on page 28)

00110101001010011101011010101010101100101000001

Samuel Morse, Inventor of the Telegraph

Samuel Finley Breese Morse (1791–1872) designed and developed the first successful single-wire electromagnetic telegraph system. Born on April 27, 1791, in Charlestown, Massachusetts, the eldest son of Reverend Jedidiah Morse and Elizabeth Ann Breese, Morse was a temperamental child. His parents enrolled him at Phillips Academy in Andover, Massachusetts, at the age of seven, where he excelled in drawing and became interested in the developing subject of electricity. Young Morse graduated from Yale College in 1810, wishing to pursue a career in art; however, this was met with strong disapproval from Jedidiah. Instead, Morse took a job as a clerk in a neighborhood bookstore and continued to paint. After a year, the elder Morse reversed his decision, and Samuel traveled to England, where he worked with the well-respected American artist Benjamin West at the Royal Academy.

Upon his return to the United States in 1815, Morse, who was now a portrait artist, opened a studio in Boston, Massachusetts. However, he soon learned that although his work attracted a lot of attention it did not sell and portrait assignments were extremely difficult to secure. Morse maintained his interest in invention and took out three patents for pumps with his brother Sidney in 1817. Morse moved to New York in 1825, where he ran for mayor twice, but was defeated. In 1826, he founded and became the first president of the National Academy of Design, an organization whose goal was to assist artists in selling their work and improve public awareness of artists' accomplishments. However, these were difficult years for Morse. He lost his wife in 1825, his father in 1826, and his mother in 1828. In 1829, he left for Europe.

On his return to New York in 1832, he was to assume the position of professor of painting and sculpture at the City University of New York. However, on the trip home, Morse encountered Charles Thomas Jackson, an inventor, who used the length of the voyage to discuss a variety of scientific topics, including electromagnetism. Jackson insisted that an electric impulse could be carried along a long wire. The idea of transmitting information over electromagnetic wire caught Morse's interest, and he sketched some models of such a device while still aboard the ship. These rough sketches outlined the three basic components of what would later become a telegraph: a sender, which opened and closed the electric circuit; a receiver, which recorded the signal using an electromagnet; and a code, which translated the electric impulse into numbers and letters. Although a working telegraph was built in 1774, it was an unwieldy machine, requiring 26 separate wires to send messages, one

00110101001010011101011010101010101100101000001

for each letter of the alphabet. A five-wire model was later built by German engineers, but Morse was determined to narrow the number of wires down to one. Morse built a model of his one-wire telegraph in 1837 that produced an EKG-like line on ticker tape, which required translation into numbers and letters. He invited F. O. J. Smith, Leonard Gale, a science professor at New York University, and Alfred Vail to be his partners in further development of the telegraph, and together they applied for a patent to protect their invention. They also worked on improving Morse's original model, that now used a dot-and-dash code to represent letters and numbers. This system had the advan-

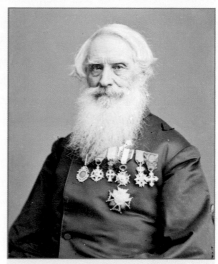

Samuel F. B. Morse, the inventor of the telegraph and Morse code
(Library of Congress)

tage of not needing to be decoded but could be instead read by operators once transmitted. The dot-and-dash code became standard all over the world.

In 1843, Congress allocated $30,000 to the construction of an experimental telegraph line between the District of Columbia and Baltimore, Maryland. On May 24, 1844, the first telegraph message was sent from the chamber of the Supreme Court to the Mount Clair train depot, which read: "What hath God wrought!" The telegraph was patented in Morse's name alone in 1854.

Morse wanted to sell his rights to the new invention to the federal government, but his plan was met with a distinct lack of interest. Instead, private companies built telegraph lines using Morse's patent, crisscrossing the country with 23 miles (37 km) of telegraph wire by 1854. The East and West Coasts of the United States were linked by telegraph wire in 1861. Morse remained president of the National Academy of Design until 1845. In 1847, he built an Italian-style mansion called Locust Grove, in Poughkeepsie, New York, which is now the Samuel Morse Historic Site. In his later years, Morse immersed himself in charitable works, including being one of the founders of Vassar College in 1861. He lived largely from the income he derived from telegraph companies' usage of his patents. Morse died on April 2, 1872, in New York City.

(continued from page 25)
content of the Web site back to the computer that requested it. This return information travels back through a series of routers and/or switches (though not necessarily the same ones that were traversed to reach the Amazon site initially) until it reaches the requesting computer. Although such a system may seem less efficient than merely transmitting information directly from the sender to recipient, one benefit of this scheme is that even if one or more routers and switches become disabled or inaccessible, network traffic can still reach its destination by being rerouted to alternative routers and switches, even if doing so slows down communication slightly.

Wireless networking is one of the latest advancements in computer networking technology. A *wireless network* is a network connected by radio waves instead of wires. Wireless networking technologies include *Bluetooth,* Wi-Fi, and *mobile broadband* technology. These technologies differ in a variety of ways, such as how they establish connections between devices and the maximum distances over which they can transmit data. As a result, each typically is used for particular purposes. Bluetooth is used for connecting peripheral devices (such as keyboards, mice, and telephone headsets) to computers no more than a few feet away; Wi-Fi is used for connecting computers to high-speed Internet connections up to a few hundred feet away; and mobile broadband is used for connecting cellular telephones to towers up to a few miles away. In all cases, once a wireless connection is established between a computing device (such as a desktop computer) and its point of access to the network (such as a wireless router), the computing device may communicate wirelessly with its access point using antennas on both devices until the connection is terminated. Although in the early years of wireless networking it was often necessary for the user to perform a series of steps to connect a computing device to a wireless network, today many computing devices are capable of automatically detecting any wireless networks in their vicinity and of automatically connecting to such networks without any action on the part of the user.

Wireless network communication is inherently slower and less reliable than wired network communication. As a result, at first many businesses and home computer users opted to connect their computers directly to a wired network when one was available, despite the added inconvenience. However, the speed and reliability of wireless networks has increased significantly in recent years.

For example, the wireless communication standard sometimes referred to as *Wireless N* can, in theory, enable wireless communications of up to 54 megabits per second, which is significantly faster than the 10 megabits per second wired connections found in most homes. Even speeds of five megabits per second are more than sufficient for sending and receiving e-mail and browsing simple Web sites. As a result, many users now rely exclusively on wireless networking and have discarded their cables in exchange for the significantly increased convenience and flexibility that wireless communication offers.

CONCLUSIONS

For most of human history, people have communicated face-to-face. Although technologies for communicating in writing have existed for thousands of years, for most of that time writing represented only a small fraction of human communication because few had the education to take advantage of it or the financial resources to purchase pen and paper, a *printing press,* or other writing tools. The last 100 years have witnessed an explosion not only in the variety, flexibility, and speed of communication technology, but also in the education and skills needed for most people to make productive use of such technology. As a result, more people are communicating with a larger number and wider variety of other people using a greater diversity of communication technology than at any other time.

When a new communication technology is invented, people tend to use it in ways in which they are familiar. The first television programs resembled plays performed on a stage, with the camera fixed on a single scene for several minutes at a time. Only later, particularly once it became possible to prerecord shows, did writers and directors realize that the new technology made it possible to tell stories in new ways, such as by cutting quickly from one scene to another, thereby escaping the limitations of the stage. Similarly, when people first had access to e-mail they tended to write e-mail messages in the same way that they wrote letters—with formal salutations, fully formed sentences, and formal paragraphs. Then, as e-mail users became familiar with the ability of e-mail messages to be transmitted, received, and read quickly, they began to trade formality for convenience, writing short messages that resembled spoken sentences more than structured essays.

Over time, creative people discovered ways to use communication technology differently from their intended uses. Many developing countries that were too poor to develop extensive land-based telephone networks have leapfrogged over such first-generation technology, skipping directly to cellular telephone networks. Although people in these countries use cell phones to talk with their friends and family, they also make more pragmatic use of modern technology. Wives, responsible for obtaining water for their families, call their relatives at the river several miles away to determine whether water is available that day, saving themselves the half-day round-trip on foot that was unavoidable before such instant communication arrived. Farmers call local markets to identify customers for their crops without needing to travel from one location to the next. Customers of small businesses use their cell phones to make payments for goods. Local officials use text messages to warn residents of impending storms. As these examples illustrate, developments in communication technology can do more than just enable people to engage in the same kinds of communication more quickly, easily, and inexpensively; they can provide people with new opportunities for improving their daily lives.

2

PERSONAL COMMUNICATION: STAYING IN TOUCH WITH FRIENDS AND FAMILY

When people lived, worked, and played in small towns, never venturing far from their own homes and communities, there was little need to use technology—even writing—to communicate. Talking to a neighbor, parent, or friend was as easy as walking down the street or shouting across a field. Only the wealthy few, who owned multiple homes and traveled to different towns or countries for extended periods, and those enlisted in the military or employed on ships at sea had a need to write letters to stay in touch with others. Even nomads, who traveled across great distances, did so with their entire families or tribes and therefore could rely solely on oral forms of communication.

This began to change in the Industrial Age, as adults began to work in factories and other facilities outside the home rather than on the family farm and as children began to work for a living or reside in boarding schools for extended periods of time. Families and communities became further separated during the great waves of immigration during the late 19th and early 20th centuries. Often, a few family members or even a single parent would venture across the Atlantic Ocean to secure work in the United States and save enough money to transport the rest of the family so that everyone could be reunited, months or even years later. The trend has continued, as children often move far from their families to attend school or find work, parents move to enjoy their retirement, and friends separate to pursue their own interests, careers, and families. Such separation can be exacerbated by wars, natural disasters, and other calamities that force people to separate for long periods of time against their will.

Most people, even those who voluntarily move far from home, desire some way to continue to stay in touch despite the physical distances. One solution is to visit in person, but doing so is slow, expensive, and complicated, especially if a meeting with many people is desired. As a result, most people increasingly are turning to electronic forms of communication to stay in touch with friends and family, using technologies such as e-mail, text messaging, video conferencing, and social networking sites. The widespread availability of low-cost, lightweight, high-speed mobile computing devices with always-on, high-speed Internet connections has made it possible for groups of friends who are separated from each other by hundreds or thousands of miles to chat with each other throughout the day as if they were all together in the same room. This chapter explores the history and current state of these and other technologies for enabling personal communication and the wide variety of ways in which they are being used.

TELEPHONE

A telephone enables two or more people who are separated over a potentially unlimited distance to speak in real time. The word *telephone* essentially means "sound at a distance" (*tele* means "distance" and *phone* means "sound"). Although this concept seems simple to us now, at first the function and capabilities of the telephone were misunderstood. The idea of a telephone was so strange, in fact, that when Alexander Graham Bell described it as a "speaking telephone" or a "talking telegraph," people inquired whether the device could speak in numbers or in a foreign language. They assumed, in other words, that the device itself could speak, not that its purpose was to transmit the speech of one person to another. This confusion may have been understandable in light of the difficulty of using the earliest telephones, which combined a transmitter and receiver into a single device that acted as both an earpiece and a mouthpiece. Holding a conversation using such a telephone required speaking into the device, then quickly moving it to one's ear to listen for the other speaker's response, and then moving it back again to one's mouth to speak again.

Despite this difficulty, the telephone was in high demand immediately after it was announced to the public. Even before the Bell Telephone Company officially opened in July 1877, 200 customers had already signed up for their own telephones. The first customers leased, rather than purchased, the first telephones, which operated over telegraph lines, for $20 a year for personal use or $40 a year for business use. The total cost of using a telephone, however, was much higher than that, because to speak to someone by telephone it was necessary for a wire to connect the two phones directly to each other. The process of installing such a wire was time-consuming and expensive and needed to be repeated for each pair of phones. As a result, only government agencies, universities, and large businesses leased phones in the first years after they became available.

This problem of high cost and complexity of connecting many telephones was eventually solved by creating telephone exchanges—offices where telephone lines were connected to a switchboard. Instead of connecting telephones directly, each telephone in a particular town was connected to a switchboard, which might

Before automatic telephone circuit switches were invented for connecting a phone caller to the phone of the person being called, human telephone operators were employed to manually connect the two parties by plugging cables on a switchboard into plugs corresponding to the parties' phones. This photograph shows such operators at work in the 1950s.   *(Stock Connection Blue/Alamy)*

be located at the center of town. This made it possible for someone using any one of the telephones connected to the switchboard to call any of the other telephones connected to the switchboard, even though no two phones were connected to each other in advance. To make a call using one of the telephones, a person would pick up the phone and an operator located at the central switchboard would answer. The caller would tell the switchboard operator which telephone number he wanted to call, and in response the switchboard operator would connect a cable from one plug on the switchboard—connected to the caller's phone—to another plug on the switchboard—connected to the callee's phone. This would complete an electrical circuit between the two telephones for the duration of the call. The operator would cause the callee's phone to ring. When the callee picked up, the operator would hang up and the caller and callee could speak to each other over the temporary connection made through the switchboard.

Such early switchboards represented a significant advance, which made telephones much more flexible because anyone in a local calling area could call anyone else within the same local calling area. Such early manual switches later became automatic and then computerized, thereby eliminating the need for switchboard operators. The theory behind today's fully automated worldwide systems, however, remains essentially the same as in the first manual systems.

The telephone had its greatest impact on personal communication after Bell's original telephone patents expired in 1893 and 1894. This made it possible for other companies, such as Western Union, to enter the telephone market, spurring competition and quickly causing telephone networks to connect major cities. However, two customers could only speak to each other by telephone if they used the same telephone company. This made it difficult to make long-distance telephone calls because Bell Company's long-distance division, American Telephone and Telegraph (AT&T), controlled all long-distance lines. By 1914, when AT&T first made coast-to-coast calls possible, it had merged with Western Union and allowed independent companies to use its long-distance lines. By this time, competition had lowered rates, which made the telephone affordable for the average person. As a result, the telephone became a common device used in everyday life. Neighbors called neighbors (even though they could talk to each other face-to-face simply by walking next door), people scheduled deliveries by telephone, and parents away from home could call home to check on their children. The most important change for many people was the ability to talk to friends and family living far away. People no longer had to travel hours to visit one another, and telephone communication was quicker than mail.

Today, the cellular telephone has transformed people's lives. Long-distance calls, even across countries, have become relatively inexpensive due to the use of cellular telephones (cell phones). Cell phone users generally are not charged for calls based on distance but use allotted minutes in a calling plan to make calls. Cellular phones also provide features such as daily planners, e-mail and Web access, and text messaging, often for additional fees. Perhaps the most significant advantage of cell phones is that they enable calls to be made and received wirelessly from any location, so long as the phone is within range of a cell phone tower. As a result, many people now use only a single cell phone account and phone number for all of their personal communications, instead of maintaining separate numbers for different

Telephone technology has advanced exponentially since the days of the rotary-dial telephone and the human-operated switchboard. This iPhone 4, which fits in a shirt pocket, can act not only as a telephone but also as an all-purpose communication device that is more powerful than many desktop computers from just a few years ago. New features can be added to the iPhone and other smartphones by installing new software applications, known as apps. *(UPI/ Apple/Landov)*

residences and changing phone numbers each time they move. This reduces the total cost of phone communication and reduces the likelihood that friends and family will be unable to find each other. These and other features of cell phones make it easier to manage one's life and to communicate with friends, family, and business contacts at any time.

E-MAIL

In 1971, computer engineer, Ray Tomlinson (1941–), invented e-mail, also known as electronic mail. Tomlinson was working for Bolt, Beranek and Newman (BBN), the company hired to work on the U.S. Internet project called ARPANET (an acronym for Advanced Research Projects Agency Network). ARPANET, created in 1969, was composed of a simple network of computers that allowed users to leave messages for one another on a single computer by using the electronic mail program called SNDMSG (an abbreviation of "send message"). Tomlinson used a file-transfer program called CPYNET (an abbreviation of "copy network") to create a new program that allowed users to send messages to one another from any computer in the network. Tomlinson's first message to users contained information about how to use the @ sign, which Tomlinson decided should be used to separate the login name from the computer host name. This use of the @ sign remains valid in e-mail addresses today.

Universities and companies also began using a system that allowed users to send messages to others in the same network. By the late 1970s and early 1980s, companies such as IBM and Apple created personal computers that were capable of sending e-mail messages. Just like the limitations placed on customers of different telephone networks, users of these early systems could only send remote messages to subscribers of the same dial-up service. Sending messages in this way was typically unreliable. The development of *local area networks* (LANs) within government agencies led to the creation of e-mail systems that were more reliable and capable of sending attachments. At first, the Internet grew from a system used only by the U.S. military to one used by universities and private corporations. Then, in the 1990s, e-mail became widely available to consumers through commercial Internet service providers, such as AOL, CompuServe, Juno, and AT&T.

To send an e-mail message, it is necessary to sign in to an e-mail account online or to run e-mail *client* software such as Microsoft Outlook or Apple Mail. The user then selects a "new message" command to generate an empty e-mail form. The user fills in the "to" section of the form with the recipient's e-mail address and types the topic of the message in the "subject" line. The user then types the text of the e-mail message into the body of the e-mail form and hits "send" when finished composing the message to cause the e-mail message to be sent to the recipient.

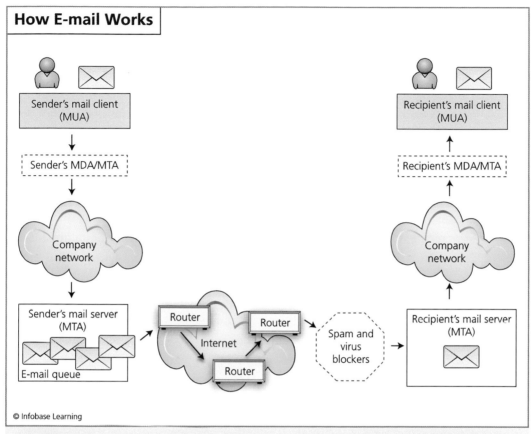

How E-mail Works

Sender's mail client (MUA)

Sender's MDA/MTA

Company network

Sender's mail server (MTA)

E-mail queue

Router

Router

Internet

Router

Spam and virus blockers

Recipient's mail client (MUA)

Recipient's MDA/MTA

Company network

Recipient's mail server (MTA)

© Infobase Learning

Although sending an e-mail message only requires the sender to type the message and click a button, a variety of software and hardware is required to successfully transmit the message from the sender's computer to the recipient's computer.

Behind the scenes, a variety of technologies work together to transmit an e-mail message from its author to its recipient. The Web browser, e-mail client (such as Outlook or Mail) or other software that the sender uses to compose the e-mail message are referred to as a *mail user agent (MUA)*. The sender's MUA provides the outgoing e-mail message to a *mail transfer agent (MTA),* which may be implemented within the sender's MUA or in separate software or hardware at the sender's location. The sender's MTA transmits the e-mail message to the sender's *mail server*. If the sender's computer is part of a LAN or other corporate network, then the e-mail message may pass through the corporate network before being received by the sender's mail server.

The sender's mail server then transmits the e-mail message over the Internet. Often the sender's mail server is connected to many computers within the sender's network and is responsible for sending e-mail on behalf of all of those computers. As a result, it may not be possible for the sender's mail server to forward every message it receives immediately, so it places outgoing e-mail messages in a queue and then transmits each message from the queue on a first-come, first-served basis as quickly as possible.

The e-mail message is forwarded from one router to another within the Internet until it reaches the mail server of the e-mail message's recipient. At this point, the recipient's network may scan the incoming e-mail message using spam and virus blockers and block the e-mail message from being delivered to the recipient if the e-mail message is determined to be spam or contain a virus. Assuming that the e-mail message is free of any such problems, a mail server in the recipient's network (another example of an MTA) forwards the message (through the recipient's corporate network, if there is such a network) to a *message delivery agent (MDA)* in the recipient's network. The recipient's MDA then provides the e-mail message to the recipient's MUA (i.e., Microsoft Outlook or Apple Mail), where the recipient can read the e-mail message. In practice, a single piece of software, such as Microsoft Outlook, may include all of the features of the MUA, MDA, and MTA, so that separate pieces of software do not need to be installed on the sender and recipient's computers.

Although most people with e-mail accounts now take Internet connections for granted, as recently as the 1980s most did not have an e-mail address or access to the Internet. In the early days of the Internet, accessing one's personal e-mail typically required using a computer connected to a dial-up modem connected to a conventional analog telephone line. Such modems were not constantly connected to the Internet. Instead, to check one's e-mail, it was necessary to initiate an Internet connection using the modem, a process that typically took 30–60 seconds to complete. One could then send and receive e-mail over the connection. One could not, however, make or receive telephone calls over the same telephone line at the same time. Therefore, people generally connected to the Internet for short periods of time and then disconnected.

Today's broadband digital modems, such as DSL modems and cable modems, are not only many times faster than yesterday's analog modems, they also do not interfere with telephone calls or television programming provided over the same wires. As a result, people with broadband modems typically keep them connected for long periods so they can check e-mail, browse the Web, and engage in other activities over the Internet without having to wait until a connection is established. Furthermore, the advent of broadband wireless Internet connections using home-based wireless network access points and hot spots in public facilities such as airports, coffee shops, universities, and libraries provides people with access to e-mail from almost anywhere. Users can now access e-mail not only through desktop and laptop computers but through mobile handheld devices such as cellular telephones and personal digital assistants (PDAs). E-mail is available through popular Web sites such as Yahoo! Mail, Windows Live Hotmail, Gmail, and AOL Mail.

Although e-mail is the oldest form of Internet-based communication, its use continues to rise steadily. In 1997, 2.7 trillion e-mail messages were dispatched, while 294 billion e-mails were sent each day in 2010. Perhaps not surprisingly, younger Internet users have been quick to adopt newer forms of Internet-based communication, such as instant messaging and text messaging, while e-mail remains the most popular form of communication among adults. According to a December 2010 study by Pew Internet and American Life, 92 percent of all adult Internet users use e-mail to send or receive text-based messages over the Internet.

INSTANT MESSENGER AND CHAT

It is no longer necessary to use the telephone to engage in immediate communication with others. Instant messaging and chat are two ways in which people communicate with each other in real time over the Internet using a keyboard or keypad. The primary feature of such forms of communication is that when one person types a message, usually a single sentence, other users engaged in the same conversation can see the message immediately, unlike e-mail, which requires people to download new e-mail into their inbox and then open the new e-mail to read it.

Various people working in universities and research organizations created chat programs in the early 1960s. The first chat programs only supported use by people connected to the same computer and only two users at a time could communicate. Later programs began to support multiple users, but only those connected to the same computer network.

Today, chat technology supports communication with multiple users simultaneously without the need for those users to be connected to the same local area network (LAN). In fact, any two users connected anywhere on the Internet can chat with each other using technologies such as *Internet relay chat (IRC)*. IRC users communicate with multiple people about specific topics in channels that reside on servers stationed around the world. Anyone who subscribes to a particular channel can post messages to that channel and view all other messages posted to that channel.

Because IRC uses a *client-server* model, users of IRC must install IRC client software on their computers and log into an IRC server before they can send or receive IRC messages. Once logged in to a server, a user can send a message in a channel by typing the message on a keyboard. The user's client software then transmits the message to the IRC server to which the user is connected. The message may be forwarded from the initial server to other servers until it finally reaches the client software of each person subscribed to the channel. Others connected to the channel may choose to read and respond to the message.

Instant messaging (IM) is another popular form of real-time chat available over the Internet. The current instant messaging programs are descendants of Bulletin Board Systems (BBSs) that were popular in the 1980s and early 1990s. Bulletin boards allowed users to download and upload data, exchange messages through message boards and e-mail, and read news and bulletins. Years later, the company Mirabilis invented the first modern instant messaging service called ICQ (pronounced "I seek you") in 1996. Shortly thereafter, AOL Instant Messenger, MSN Messenger, and Yahoo! Messenger were released. The latest IM technology also allows users to communicate by video conferencing, Web conferencing, and using mobile devices.

Instant messaging services, such as AOL Instant Messenger (AIM), are accessed using client software installed on a computer. Once a user logs on to the messaging service, the AIM server establishes a connection to the client software on the user's computer. The service allows users to create a contact list (sometimes called a "friend list" or "buddy list") that notifies users when people on the list are logged in to the AIM server. Anyone logged in to an AIM server can send messages to people on their contact list. The AIM server routes such messages to their recipients immediately, where the messages are displayed immediately. Instant messaging, therefore, is used by people when they want to communicate with each other by text in a manner similar to that of a voice telephone call, in which both parties can freely communicate back and forth without delay. More than two people can communicate over a single instant messaging session simultaneously, much like an old telephone party line.

Because instant messaging and chat rely on the use of the keyboard to create messages, and typing is time-consuming, these forms of communication have led to new forms of writing that use keystrokes as efficiently as possible to express emotions and common words. For example, many abbreviations that originated in the world of chat, such as LOL (which means "laugh out loud"), are now recognized universally. The desire to send even shorter messages has led to the popularity of services such as Twitter, which only allows messages of 140 characters or fewer. Besides the ease of communicating in abbreviated form, IM and chat provide the benefit of instantaneous communication that is unavailable in e-mail. E-mail, while less formal than letter writing, does require the writer to put more thought into the communication. IM and chat users tend to write in a more carefree style.

USENET

Usenet is a worldwide electronic discussion forum comprised of thousands of discussion forums, referred to as *newsgroups,* each of which is related to a particular topic. The Duke University graduates Tom Truscott and Jim Ellis created Usenet in 1980. The purpose of the service was to allow the exchange of text content, such as mailing lists and news feeds, between users. The service began with three machines that were set up in North Carolina.

Newsgroups are organized into a hierarchical system of categories, subcategories, subcategories of subcategories, and so on. Categories include recreation (rec.*), humanities (humanities.*), miscellaneous (misc.*), news (news.*), science (sci.*), society (soc.*), controversial topics (talk.*), and computers (comp.*). Although special newsgroup software is necessary to view and respond to discussions, referred to as threads, in recent years such software has been incorporated within standard Web browsers and e-mail clients.

Some newsgroups are moderated, which means that a human moderator reads each message before it is posted. In such newsgroups, the moderator may decide that a particular message is unfit for posting and decide not to post it as a result. In unmoderated newsgroups, all messages are posted automatically without any review. In both moderated and unmoderated newsgroups, messages are posted to a newsgroup server. Once posted, a message may be duplicated onto other newsgroup servers to make it easier for users around the world to access as many newsgroups as possible.

Users subscribe to newsgroups covering topics that interest them. Once a user is subscribed to one or more newsgroups, the user's newsgroup software downloads new messages in the subscribed newsgroups from the newsgroup server at the user's ISP so that the user may read some or all of the messages. The user may post responses to existing messages or create a new thread containing its own messages. Although sending and receiving newsgroup messages is similar in some ways to sending and receiving e-mail messages, the primary difference is that newsgroup messages are directed to a particular newsgroup covering a particular topic, whereas e-mail messages are directed to one or more specific individuals whose e-mail addresses are listed in the "To" field of the message.

The original function of Usenet has been largely superseded over the years by other communication methods, such as Web forums, mailing lists, and social networking Web sites. In recent years, newsgroups have become more frequently used as a way for people to transfer large binary files to each other, since such files are often impossible to transfer using e-mail due to their size and other characteristics. Binary files are typically converted into a text-based format using software such as uuencode, MIME, or yEnc, before uploading the file to a newsgroup. Anyone may then subscribe to the newsgroup to download the file and then use similar software to convert the file back into its original binary format. This use of newsgroups, however, has led to the widespread unlawful transfer of copyrighted material, such as movies and video games, without permission from copyright holders. As a result, large copyright holders, such as film studios and record labels, often monitor newsgroups for postings of copyrighted works.

BLOGS

The term *Web log* was originally coined by Jorn Barger in 1997 to refer to a Web page that contained postings listed in reverse chronological order (i.e., from newest to oldest). Web log was eventually shortened by programmer Peter Merholz in 1999 into the term *blog*. Blogs are used as personal diaries or as vehicles for commentary on politics, sports, popular culture, and other topics. Many blogs include links to resources on the Web site or to other sites. College student Justin Hall wrote one of the earliest blogs in 1994, entitled simply, "Justin's Home Page." This blog was a diary that included text, video, and photographs. Dave Winer launched one of the oldest blogs, called Scripting News, in 1997. Scripting News was a news page for Frontier Software customers, containing announcements related to the company's software.

These and other early blogs represented a new way of using webpages. Before blogs, many webpages were used to store and display static (unchanging) information, such as conference papers and encyclopedia entries. Other webpages, such as those provided by newspapers and magazines, provided updated content periodically, but every time new content was provided, it replaced the old content. If one visited the *New York Times* home page one day and then the next day, the previous day's articles would no longer be on the home page and could only be accessed by searching for them. In contrast, the reverse-chronological format of blogs provided a useful vehicle for providing updated information, while still making it easy to find and view older information simply by scrolling down the page.

Another benefit of blogs is that they are easier to write and maintain than traditional Web sites. At first, however, writing a blog required some technical skill at Web site design. In 1999, Pyra Labs released Blogger, a free blogging service that made it easier to create and update blogs without any technical knowledge. Now many such services exist. Every year, blogs continued to increase in popularity as other companies created blogging software. Today, blogs are still used as personal diaries, but blogs are also used by corporations, news services, teachers, churches, and by countless others for a variety of purposes.

Blogging is an easy and simple way to communicate with users on a Web site. The first blogs required manual updates, but the creation of browser-based software now makes it easy for nontechnical users because updates are automatic. To create a blog, the user logs in to the blogging software. To create a new post using the WordPress service, for example, the user would select "new post" from the main page. The user then inputs the title and main body of the *post* by typing them. To add a link the user highlights the selection for the link and then selects the link button. The entire process resembles that of writing a document using a word processor.

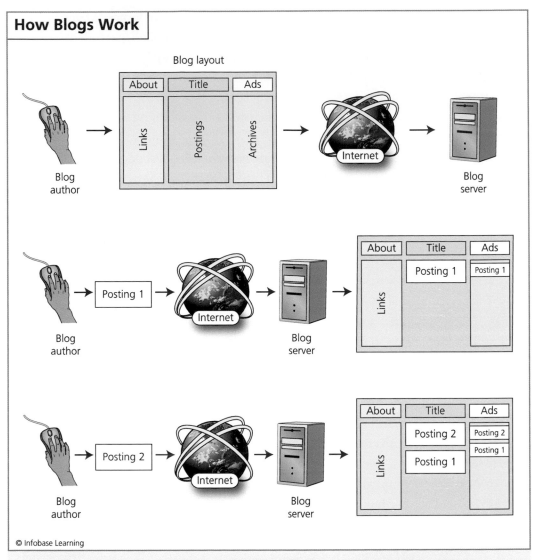

How Blogs Work

Blog layout

Blog author

About | Title | Ads
Links | Postings | Archives

Internet

Blog server

Blog author

Posting 1

Internet

Blog server

About | Title | Ads
Links | Posting 1 | Posting 1

Blog author

Posting 2

Internet

Blog server

About | Title | Ads
Links | Posting 2 | Posting 2
Posting 1
Posting 1

At the heart of all blogs is software that enables the blog's author to update the blog with new postings quickly and easily, so that the author does not need to manually edit the blog Webpage. When a blog author posts a new blog entry, most blogging software will both insert the new entry into the blog webpage at an appropriate location and also make other updates to the webpage automatically, such as adding the new entry to a chronological list of entries on the side of the page.

Once created, blog posts are stamped with a date and time and displayed in reverse chronological order. The first post displayed is the most recent and is followed by an archive of prior posts. A published blog post contains a heading, a date and time stamp, the text of the blog post itself, and a list of any comments written by readers of the blog post. This ability for readers of the blog to post their own comments directly to the blog is one of the most popular features of blogs and helps blog authors keep their readers engaged.

A blogger may allow other Web sites or users to redistribute blog post- ings through an *RSS* feed (an acronym for *Really Simple Syndication* or Rich Site Summary). A blogger can allow other sites to publish some of its content

Twitter

Twitter is a free social networking and microblogging service used to send real- time short messages to others. The idea for Twitter emerged during a board mem- ber brainstorming session for the San Francisco, California, podcasting company Odeo. Jack Dorsey's idea was based on the concept of staying in touch with what his friends were doing. In March 2006, a prototype was built and the first mes- sage, "just setting up my twttr," was sent by Dorsey. Odeo employees used Twitter until its release to the public in August 2006. Twitter quickly rose in popularity and had more than 56 million active users in 2011.

Twitter users can send and receive messages through Twitter.com or by *SMS (Short Message Service),* using a computer, cell phone, tablet computer, or any other device connected to the Internet. The service requires the user to create a profile with a maximum of 160 characters. Once registered, a user can begin send- ing messages. A message, also known as a tweet, is sent by using @ followed by the user's name. The recipient of a tweet is known as a follower. Tweets are limited to 140 characters and can be sent in real time to all followers or just to an individual follower. Because Twitter provides a way to update friends and family, it is not nec- essary to respond to a tweet. Tweets can be delivered immediately or the service can be set to automatically download the recipient's tweets at a specific time.

Twitter was designed to shorten online communication, while at the same time creating a way for people to stay connected. Tweets may include information about simple functions or provide real-time information about emergencies. In January 2009, a ferry passenger located near the U.S. Airways plane that crashed in the Hudson River used Twitter to upload a picture and comment about the accident prior to the arrival of traditional news organizations.

by registering with an RSS publisher for distribution through an RSS feed. RSS feeds contain the headline, a summary, and the Web site source.

The most popular blogging services include Blogger, BlogSpot, WordPress, TypePad, and Windows Live Space. WordPress is an easy-to-use free blogging service that is suitable for amateur and experienced bloggers. It features customization of templates, a variety of plugins and widgets, and statistics. TypePad is a fee service that provides different features depending upon a subscriber's subscription. It provides a variety of layouts, has a feed service, and does not place advertisements on the user's site. The Windows Live Space is a free blog service that is part of a personal Web page. The page is called a "Space," on which the user may publish text and pictures and create a personal profile and list of friends. Blogging services differ from each other primarily in the degree of technical expertise needed to create and maintain a blog, in the variety of advanced features they provide, and in their price. The result is a marketplace of blogging products and services to fit almost any type of blogger.

VIDEO AND AUDIO COMMUNICATIONS

Within just a few years after the patent on the first telephone in 1876, imaginations soared about the creation of a telephone with video capabilities. The telephonoscope was a telephone combined with a wide-screen television. Years later in 1927, AT&T created the first electro-mechanical videophone. It required so much equipment that it could easily occupy multiple cabinets. One of the videophone's first uses was by commerce secretary Herbert Hoover to make a call from Washington, D.C., to New York. The videophone had two-way audio and one-way video so that although those on the line in New York could see and hear Hoover, Hoover could only hear them.

In 1956, AT&T introduced a prototype of its videophone called Picturephone. In 1964, AT&T marketed the videophone at Disneyland and at the World's Fair in New York. Special exhibits allowed people to try the videophone by placing calls between videophone booths. AT&T quickly discovered that people did not like the phones because of the bulky equipment, small screen, and controls that were difficult to use. Nevertheless, AT&T continued to work on developing the videophone. In 1970, a commercial Picturephone service opened in Pittsburgh. Although AT&T predicted that 1 million videophones would be in use in 10 years, their large size and the expense deterred consumers.

The technology at the time was inadequate for videophones. Connecting two videophones served by the same central office was possible by using three standard telephone wire pairs. While one pair connected the 1 MHz video signal in one direction, the second pair of wires carried the video signal in the other direction, and the third pair carried the two-way voice call and the tone dialing. A videophone connection from one central office to another was more complicated. At the time, a voice channel was capable of 3,000 Hz, but a videophone needed 1 million Hz. Consequently, it would only take a few videophone calls to use all of the available bandwidth.

Although videophones were at first impracticable, the introduction of new technology in the 1990s led to the emergence of AT&T's VideoPhone 2500, the first color videophone. It was capable of working over low-bandwidth analog telephone lines because it used digital compression to reduce the bandwidth requirement. The device used a modem to transmit the video signal over the telephone line that was received and sent through the central office switches. The VideoPhone cost $1,500 and transmitted at 19.2 kilobits per second if the quality of the line was good or at 16.8 kilobits per second over a poor line. Despite the technological advancements of the videophone, it was discontinued in 1995 after experiencing dismal sales.

With the introduction of computers and the Internet, video and audio communication has become possible without a videophone. Video calls can be conducted in real time across the Internet with anyone around the world. Services such as Skype, paired with a high-speed Internet connection, a microphone, a Web cam, and speakers, are the basic tools necessary to make personal video calls. Making a successful video call requires converting the video image at one end into digital data and then compressing that data before transmitting it over the Internet. Such compression is necessary because uncompressed data would be too large to send quickly enough, even over high-speed Internet connections. The computer on the other end receives the compressed data, decompresses it, and then displays the uncompressed data on the recipient's computer. Such communication occurs simultaneously in both directions with both video and audio data so that both parties can see and hear each other simultaneously.

Today's digital cameras can both take pictures and act as communication devices by enabling photos and videos to be transmitted to others over the Internet directly from the camera using a wireless connection. *(Szymon Apanowicz/Shutterstock)*

The Internet has also made it possible to stream video over the Web. Because video files are large, in the early days of computers it was difficult and time-consuming to send a video file to someone else's computer. In particular, it was necessary to wait for the entire file to download before beginning to view. This often meant that the recipient had to wait several hours. In contrast, today's streaming video technologies compress the file so that it is smaller and easier to transmit and allow the beginning of the video to be played while the remainder of the video continues to be transmitted to the user's computer. The entire video may not ever be saved on the viewer's computer at any one time; instead, only the portion of the video currently being watched, and small buffer of a few minutes of video before and after that point, may be stored on the viewer's computer. Web sites such as YouTube allow users to post video for others to watch in streaming format. Many users on YouTube engage in video conversations by posting videos in response to the videos of others, whether minutes or days later. This has become a creative way for people to share information about a variety of subjects and to communicate with each other without the need to engage in real-time conversation or express one's thoughts in writing.

SOCIAL NETWORKING WEB SITES

Social networking Web sites create online communities where users can expand social contacts by connecting with friends, family, and strangers. Social networking initially took place on Bulletin Boards and in discussion groups, but as the Internet continued to expand in the 1990s so did ways of communicating with others. In 1997, SixDegrees launched the first notable social networking site that allowed users to create a profile, list friends, and search for acquaintances. Because building connections through the Internet was still new to most people, SixDegrees failed to engage enough users and was dismantled in 2000.

Shortly after the dating service Friendster launched in 2002, its user base soared. Friendster was based on the idea of friends introducing other friends to potential romantic matches. Friendster had trouble supporting such tremendous growth, and its restrictions on the number of allowable connections led to a decline in interest. However, the initial popularity of Friendster was an indication of the potential popularity of online social networking.

Beginning in 2003, the creation and success of social networking sites coincided with an increase in the number and diversity of Internet users. Sites such as LinkedIn, Myspace, Flickr, Facebook, and CouchSurfing emerged. Social networking sites have come to serve a wide variety of purposes. For instance, LinkedIn concentrates on creating business connections between users, Flickr is an online photo management site that allows users to upload photos and videos to share with visitors from all over the world, and CouchSurfing is a service that connects worldwide travelers with volunteers who offer free accommodations.

Facebook is the most prominent social networking Web site. In 2003, Tom Anderson and Chris DeWolfe founded MySpace (later renamed Myspace). Facebook, launched one year later by Harvard University student Mark Zuckerberg, was originally a way for university students to connect. Its instant popularity led to the expansion of the service to everyone. Facebook allows users to create a profile, build a network of friends, upload photos and videos, send and receive messages, engage in real-time chat, and search for friends. Facebook emphasizes the creation of connections based on shared interests and networks comprised

Social networking services, such as Facebook and Myspace, are available through their Web sites and apps on mobile devices. This photo shows a member of Facebook engaged in a real-time chat with another Facebook member using the Facebook app on an iPod Touch. *(TheProductGuy/ Alamy)*

of people who attend the same school or share the same employer. It offers users a personal Internet presence without the need to manually create a personal webpage. Instead, these services essentially create a dynamically updated personal webpage for each user, on which all information about that user, such as messages, photos, and interests, can be found at any time. When a user posts any new information to his or her account, such information is immediately and automatically reflected on the user's page, thereby eliminating the need for the user to have the technical knowledge necessary to design or update webpages.

Social networking sites are a primary component of a set of technological developments that have become loosely known as *Web 2.0.* The term *Web 2.0* was coined in 2003 by Internet media businessman Tim O'Reilly to refer to changes in the ways in which the Web is being used by designers and to changes in the behavior of Internet users. These included a movement from personal Web sites to blogs, from publishing to participation, from traditional encyclopedias written by experts such as Britannica Online to collaboratively written online encyclopedias such as Wikipedia, and the movement from centralized online photo services such as Ofoto to decentralized photo-sharing services such as Flickr. *User-generated content,* such as videos posted to YouTube and user reviews on Amazon.com, is also a key characteristic of Web 2.0. Another distinguishing

100111010010101010011001011101101010010101001

Ray Tomlinson, Programmer of the First E-mail Software

Raymond Samuel Tomlinson was born in 1941 in Amsterdam, New York. He graduated from Rensselaer Polytechnic Institute in Troy, New York, in 1963, with a bachelor's degree in electrical engineering and continued his education at the Massachusetts Institute of Technology (MIT), graduating in 1965 with a master's degree in electrical engineering.

After working on his doctorate for two years, in 1967 Tomlinson joined the Boston firm of Bolt Beraneck and Newman (currently BBN Technologies), where he worked on network programs, including an experimental file-transfer program

(continues)

Ray Tomlinson, widely credited as the inventor of e-mail, shown here holding an @ sign, which Tomlinson decided should be used to separate an e-mail username from its domain name. *(© Ed Quinn/Corbis)*

100111010010101010011001011101101010010101001

001101010010100111010110101010101100101000001

(continued)

called CPYNET, an early form of today's FTP (file transfer protocol). BBN had won a government contract from DARPA (Defense Advanced Research Projects Agency) to create a communication network that would enable scientists to share each other's computer facilities called ARPANET (Advanced Research Projects Agency Network), which became a precursor of the modern-day Internet. In late 1971, Tomlinson was tasked with working on a program that allowed users of the same computer to leave messages for one another called SNDMSG.

SNDMSG and other similar single-computer electronic mail have been in existence since the 1960s. These mail programs worked by allowing users to append messages to another user's mailbox (file), but protected the existing data in the file from being read or overwritten. It occurred to Tomlinson that CPYNET could be just as effective at appending messages as SNDMSG, but would allow users to send messages not just to users of the same computer, but to any user on the network. Tomlinson rewrote the CPYNET code to allow for appending, rather than sending and receiving the files, and incorporated the CPYNET code into SNDMSG. All that remained was to find a way to distinguish local mail (mail was sent from a user of one computer to another user of the same computer) from network mail (mail sent from a user of one to computer to a user of a different computer over a network). For this Tomlinson chose the @ sign, to separate the username from the host name and indicate that this was a nonlocal host, creating a username@host identifier to which a message could be sent. Tomlinson estimates that he spent no more than six hours spread over a week or two whenever he had a spare moment from working on other things.

001101010010100111010110101010101100101000001

feature of Web 2.0 is the use of tools such as the JavaScript-based *Ajax* (short for asynchronous JavaScript and XML) to enable webpages to respond to user actions, such as by displaying additional text in response to the pressing of a button by the user, without requiring the entire page to reload. Such tools have enabled webpages to behave more like fully functional and interactive software programs rather than merely as static displays of predesigned information. It is expected that Web 3.0, also known as the *Semantic Web,* will feature machines capable of reading and understanding webpages in the same way that humans

The first e-mail message sent using SNGMSG was sent between two computers that stood about 15 feet apart and were connected only by the ARPANET network. Tomlinson sent a number of test messages to himself, which he describes as forgettable and completely unremarkable, most likely containing something similar to "QWERTYUIOP" or "TESTING 1 2 3 4." Once satisfied with the way the program worked, Tomlinson sent a message to the rest of the group explaining how to use the new program. Tomlinson, however, did not make a big deal of his invention, because it was not what his team was working on. However, Larry Roberts, the director of DARPA, adopted the new messaging system as his primary means of business communication and even wrote a program that read e-mail. Soon, researchers who depended on Roberts for their funding had no choice but to get online, swelling the ranks of e-mail users.

Tomlinson chose the "@" sign because he thought it was not used with any significance by the time-sharing system on which SNDMSG relied, not commonly found in either usernames or host names, and also corresponded to the English "at," which in his mind was convenient to indicate that a user was located elsewhere on the network. Despite some misconceptions, he did not invent the @ sign, although he did elevate its profile from relative obscurity to common usage.

Tomlinson was granted the George R. Stibitz Computer Pioneer Award by the American Computer Museum in 2000, the Webby Award for Lifetime Achievement from the International Academy of Digital Arts and Sciences in 2001, was inducted into the Rensselaer Alumni Hall of Fame, and received the IEEE Internet Award in 2004. Tomlinson remains at BBN Technologies as a principal engineer, which is a position of distinction within the company.

do, which will allow searches based on natural language queries rather than keyword queries.

CONCLUSIONS

The problem described at the beginning of this chapter—how to not lose touch with friends and family over long distances—has now largely been solved, at least for people who have easy, reliable, and affordable access to the Internet.

Such technology makes it possible for people to communicate at nearly any time, from any place, and using nearly any form of communication, whether it be text, audio, video, or a combination of all three.

As is often the case, however, when new technologies are rapidly introduced and widely adopted, the solution to old problems can lead to the creation of new ones. Despite the benefits of being able to share one's latest accomplishments with family members, complain about daily problems to close friends, or simply chat about nothing in particular with acquaintances at any time, being constantly connected can be overwhelming in many ways. The sheer number of e-mail messages, text messages, voice calls, and other incoming communications that any one person receives in a single day has skyrocketed over the last decade. Failing to respond to an e-mail message quickly enough—whether that be a minute, an hour, or a day—may be viewed as an insult by the author of the message. This can create pressure to respond to every message that one receives as quickly as possible. Yet sending responses tends to elicit yet additional incoming messages. Simply staying on top of such communications at all hours of the day, without any clear boundaries or time spent offline, can be both time-consuming and stressful.

This problem is compounded by the fact that engaging in electronic communication frequently can grow addictive, detracting from other activities and other kinds of relationships. A recent study found that many families sit in separate rooms in the same home at the end of the day, with each family member using his or her own computer, cell phone, videogame system, or television, instead of sitting down together in person, even for a single meal. Children often did not even turn away from the screen for a moment to greet their mother or father arriving home from a day at work.

These are examples of the ways in which new communication technologies can trigger behaviors that are out of sync with previously held values and routines. People tend to latch on to the new features of the latest smart phone and to use such features to their fullest, as quickly and frequently as possible. For example, shortly after cell phones became widely adopted, many people began to carry their cell phones with them and to always keep them turned on so that they could easily be reached anywhere and at any time, whether for an emergency or simply out of convenience. At first, it was common for someone to answer a cell phone any time it rang, even at a quiet dinner table, during the performance of a play, or in the middle of a business meeting, despite the inter-ruption and annoyance this would cause to everyone else present. Eventually, people came to understand that this was rude and that the mere technological ability of a cell phone to be called at any time did not mean that it was socially appropriate to answer it at any time. Now, most people know to turn their cell phones off (or at least to put their ringers into "vibrate" mode) upon entering a situation in which a ringing cell phone would be disruptive to others. This is just one example of ways in which technological advances tend to drive human behavior unthinkingly and in which further corrective changes to people's habits often lag far behind in time because they require additional thought and careful reflection about the impact of technology on human relationships. Such ripple effects from the current generation of personal communication technology are likely to continue flowing for many years to come.

3

BUSINESS COMMUNICATION: BEYOND INTEROFFICE MAIL

Although businesses use many of the same communication technologies as individuals—such as telephones, e-mail software, and Web browsers—business communication differs from personal communication. Because business communication strives to increase profits in addition to conveying information, businesses need to enable their employees to communicate in particular ways that advance business goals. Also, businesses require reliability, security, quality, and speed that individuals do not need. As a result, businesses often are at the leading edge of developing and adopting new communication technologies that eventually filter down to individual computer users after the technologies become more mature and inexpensive. This chapter examines a few of the particular ways in which businesses have helped to advance communication technology and in which businesses use such technology today.

INTERNAL COMMUNICATION: NETWORKING TECHNOLOGY

As described in chapter 1, a computer network is a collection of two or more computers that are interconnected so that they can transmit information. The earliest computers could only work in isolation; they could not be networked. Networking first became possible in the 1950s with the introduction of enormous computers called *mainframes.* Users of a mainframe would not interact with it directly using a keyboard or monitor connected to the mainframe, in the way that today's computer users interact directly with their personal computers. Instead, many simple computers, referred to as *terminals,* would be connected to a single mainframe. Each terminal would have its own keyboard, monitor, and networking hardware sufficient to communicate with the mainframe. Users would sit at the terminals, which might be located a large distance from the mainframe, in a separate room or even a separate building, and access the mainframe remotely. Although it would appear that they were running software on the terminals (which were sometimes called "dumb terminals" to emphasize that all of the computing intelligence resided in the mainframe), in fact they were running software on the mainframe. The terminal was merely an interface to the mainframe, like a window into the mainframe that allowed users to see the output of the mainframe's software and to provide input to such software at a distance. Many users could work simultaneously on a single mainframe in this way from multiple terminals.

Mainframes were both large and expensive, costing government agencies, universities, and private companies hundreds of thousands of dollars to procure and maintain. Furthermore, mainframes had to be stored in air-conditioned rooms and could only be serviced by teams of experts. IBM, one of the first companies to produce mainframes, introduced the System/360 mainframe in 1964, which came to dominate the mainframe market because of its nearly unlimited storage capabilities, its ability to integrate all data processing applications into a single system, and the availability of the system to remote users. Although many mainframes have been replaced today by modern computer servers, mainframes continue to be used by government agencies and some companies. Today's mainframes are capable of supporting thousands of users simultaneously. Mainframe users today typically connect to mainframes using personal computers instead of terminals.

The introduction of personal computers in the 1970s led to technologies that enabled these computers to network directly, without the need to connect through a mainframe. Although there are many kinds of networks, two of the most common are local area networks (LANs) and *wide-area networks (WANs)*. A LAN connects computers located within close proximity of one another, usually within a single office or department in a single building.

Many LANs use a technology known as Ethernet to enable communication. Although Ethernet was originally developed by a private company, 3Com Corporation, as a commercial product, its creators eventually allowed it to be adopted as a standard that could be used by any company that manufactures networking hardware. As a result, networking products available from many companies, such as cables, routers, switches, and modems, use Ethernet, which enables all of them to communicate.

A WAN connects computers that are geographically far apart. This type of network is effective for connecting multiple offices of a single business located in separate buildings and possibly even in separate states or countries. A WAN consists of at least two LANs connected by telephone lines, radio waves, or some other means of communication. Often a business will pay a communication carrier to create such a long distance LAN-LAN connection over a "leased line." Carriers that offer this service include long-distance telephone carriers and companies that operate fiber optic networks. WAN links often travel over lines maintained by more than one carrier. The largest WAN in the world is the Internet.

One function performed by networks is to enable people to exchange files without needing to physically transport such files on disks, USB keys, or other physical storage media. In the simplest form of file sharing, one user transmits a file from one computer to another user's computer, such as by transmitting the file as an attachment to an e-mail message. Although this method of file sharing is fast and convenient, it requires the file's original owner to transmit it to the person or people who want to receive it. A more sophisticated method of file sharing involves using a *file server,* typically a computer, connected to a network, which stores a large number of files. Any user of a computer that is connected to the same network as the file server can log in to the file server over the network, download files from the file server, and upload files to the file server. File servers are commonly used in businesses and universities to enable their members to share files and to collaborate on documents across multiple computers.

Another common use of networks is to enable multiple computers to share devices such as printers and scanners. In the early days of computing, a printer could only be connected to a single computer. Therefore, if multiple users wanted to print documents, they had two options. The first was to connect a separate printer to each computer. The second option was to connect a single shared computer to a group printer and then transmit files to the shared computer—known as a *print server*—for printing. Users would then walk over to the group printer to pick up their own printouts. Both options continue to be used today, depending on the needs of the users. It is desirable to have individual printers connected to users' computers if each user require convenient printing of simple documents, which can be provided by today's low-cost desktop print-ers, but not if users require high-speed printing of complex documents (such as professional-quality photographs), which can only be provided by large, expen-sive printers, which most organizations cannot afford to purchase for every user in the organization.

Yet another common function performed by computer networks is to enable users to share software. For example, in most organizations, all users need to use the same word processing software, such as Microsoft Word. It is very tedious and time-consuming to install the same word processing software on each user's computer and to install patches and upgrades onto each computer. Most of this effort can be eliminated by installing a single copy of the word processing soft-ware on a single server computer that is accessible over a network to the indi-vidual users' computers. When a user runs the word processing software, such as by double-clicking on the Microsoft Word icon, the user's computer accesses the software from the server, even though it appears to the user as if the software is being accessed on the user's own computer. Most software companies charge a fee to businesses that use such software servers based on the number of users in the business. For example, if Microsoft sells a single copy of Microsoft Word to a business that plans to let 100 users share that copy of the software, Microsoft will charge the business for all 100 users, not merely for the single copy.

Many of the examples above involve centralized computers known as *serv-ers,* such as file servers and print servers. Server-based networks typically are most useful for organizations with at least 10 computers. For smaller organiza-tions, the time and expense required to purchase and maintain one or more servers often is not worthwhile. Instead, such organizations often use a simpler kind of network known as a *peer-to-peer network,* in which each computer con-nects relatively directly to all other computers in the network using a network device such as a switch. As a result, all computers in the network function as peers; there is no centralized control over files, printers, or software as in a *client-server system.* For example, in a peer-to-peer network, each computer typically can access files on all of the other computers in the network. Although this can lead to weaker security than in a server-based network, it results in a network that is easier and less expensive to create and maintain, and security is often not as significant a concern in smaller organizations. In practice, every organization must take into account a variety of factors, such as the number of computers, the

Corporate Network

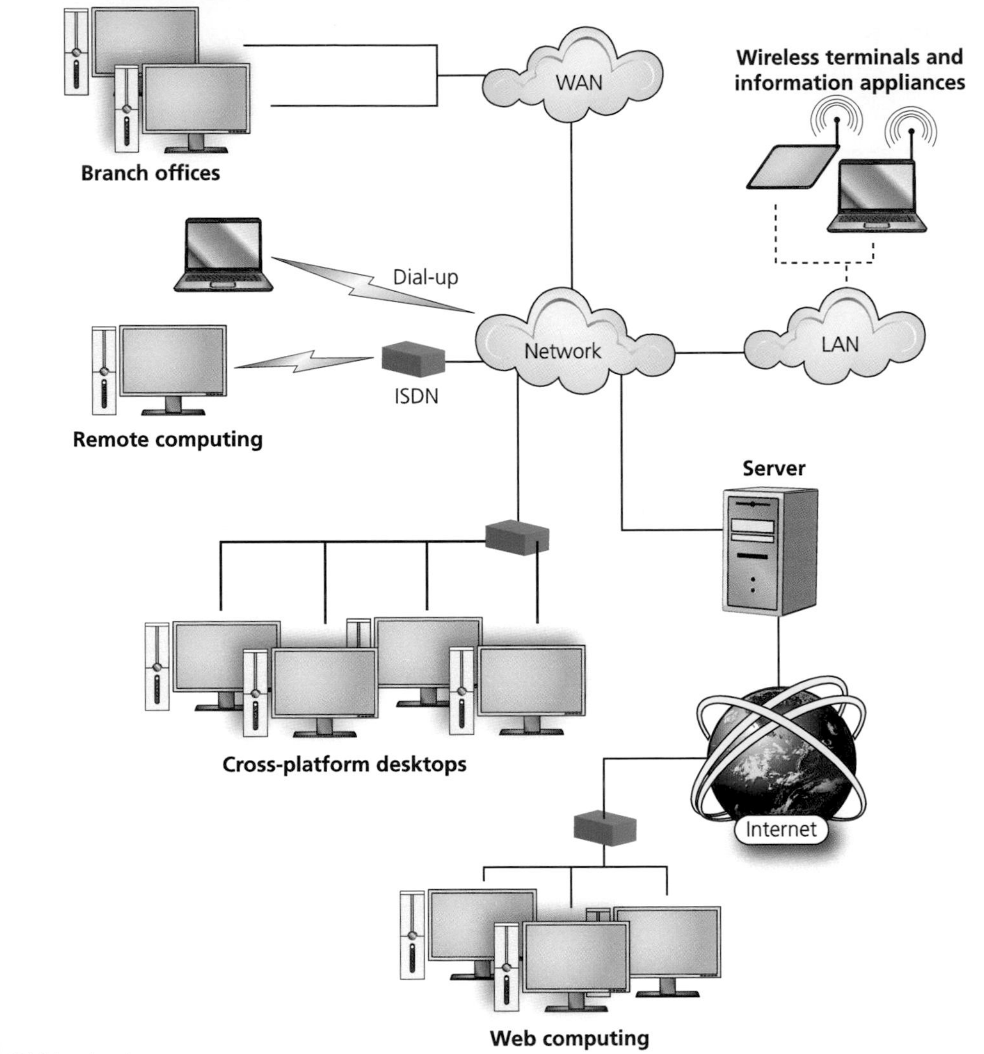

Branch offices

WAN

Wireless terminals and information appliances

Dial-up

Remote computing

ISDN

Network

LAN

Server

Cross-platform desktops

Internet

Web computing

© Infobase Learning

As a result of their larger number of users and more stringent requirements for reliability and security, corporate computer networks typically require a wider variety of networking equipment than home computer networks. This diagram illustrates a common way in which computers are connected to each other over a corporate network.

need for security, and the organization's budget when deciding which kind of network will best meet the organization's needs.

DOCUMENT SHARING AND MANAGEMENT

File sharing allows multiple users in a network to access, view, copy, print, and modify the same files. In the 1970s, people shared files by copying them onto floppy disks and then giving the disk to other users to copy the files onto their own computers. A floppy disk is device on which files can be stored in the form of electromagnetic signals using a floppy disk drive. Sharing files using floppy disks was often referred to in the computing field as "sneakernet" because after transferring the file to a diskette it was walked over to someone else's computer.

Computer networks have eliminated the need to transfer files using floppy disks, USB keys, or other physical media, by making it possible to transfer files from one computer to another directly over the network. Many companies use a hard disk drive that is shared by and made accessible to all computers on the network. As a result, if one user wants to share a document with another user, the first user can simply use his computer to store the document on the shared network drive and the second user can use her computer to open the document from the shared network drive. This eliminates the need to transmit the document from the first user to the second user using an e-mail message or any other kinds of message.

Documents on a shared network drive, however, can be difficult to organize and find, particularly when the shared drive contains millions of documents shared by hundreds or thousands of users. It can be particularly difficult for one user to find files that were created by another user, especially if the other user gave the file an unusual name or stored the file in the wrong directory. To address this problem, *document management systems* have been created for the purpose of simplifying the task of storing shared files in a way that makes them easier to search for and find. The first document management systems of the 1980s were used by businesses primarily to manage paper documents, not electronic files. As computer usage became more widespread, document management systems expanded to become capable of storing, indexing, and retrieving scanned versions of paper documents. These systems were often referred to as *electronic document management (EDM)*.

Modern content management systems can keep track of any kind of document, regardless of whether it was originally created on paper or electronically. One way in which they attempt to make finding documents easier is by storing a wide variety of information along with each document. For example, when a user first creates a word processing document and saves it, the document management system may require the user to enter not only the name of the document, but also additional metadata, such as the name of the department for which the user works, the name of the project for which the document was created, and an indication of whether the document is a draft or a completed document. The document management system may generate and store additional metadata automatically, such as the username of the user who created the document. The document management system saves all of this metadata along with the document. Then, if another user searches for all documents created by the company's marketing department, the document management system can search through the metadata of all documents stored in the system to provide the user with a list of matching documents. This makes it easier to find documents than in systems that are limited to searching for documents by properties such as filename and creation date.

Document management systems may also help users to collaborate efficiently. For example, if one user opens a document using a document management system, the system may mark the document as "checked out," and then prohibit other users from copying or editing the document until the first user is finished working on it. This prevents multiple users from creating multiple, distinct versions of the same document, a situation that can create great confusion among users about which version of the document is the most accurate and up to date.

Document management systems cannot always capture information about every document on every user's computer. For example, if a user downloads a document from the Internet, the user's document management system may not be capable of automatically incorporating information about the document into the document management system's database. As a result, if the user later performs a search for the downloaded document using the document management system, the document management system may fail to find the document because the document management system does not know that the document is on the user's computer. To address this problem, *desktop search software* such as Microsoft Windows Desktop Search and Google Desktop can be used to find files without using, or as a supplement to, a content management system. Such desktop search software continuously scans the user's computer for files and keeps a record of the files that it finds in an index. Then, when the user performs a search, the desktop search software can quickly provide the results by searching through its index, rather than by searching the user's entire hard drive from scratch. Another benefit of desktop search software and some content management systems is that users can enter a single search query to search not only within files, but also within e-mail messages, photos, chat history, and other kinds of content for the information they are trying to find.

VOICE OVER IP AND VIDEO COMMUNICATION

Voice over Internet Protocol (VoIP, often pronounced "voyp") makes it possible to make telephone calls using a broadband Internet connection, rather than by using a standard telephone line. VoIP converts the user's voice into a digital signal and then transmits the digital signal over the Internet. One way to make a VoIP call is to use a computer outfitted with a microphone, speakers, and VoIP software. Another way is to use a special VoIP phone plugged into an Internet connection device, such as a cable modem. Yet another way is to use a traditional phone equipped with a special VoIP adaptor. The caller on the receiving end can receive and engage in the call using a traditional telephone, just as if the caller had placed the call using a traditional telephone.

Companies such as Skype that provide VoIP software and that route VoIP calls through the Internet to their destination typically charge significantly lower rates than traditional telephone carriers, especially for international calls. One reason for the difference in price is that VoIP calls are routed over existing data networks, rather than over separate voice networks requiring their own support and maintenance. As a result, VoIP is becoming an increasingly common way for individuals and businesses to communicate with each other inexpensively. Basic VoIP accounts typically provide services such as free conference calling and call forwarding, which often incur additional fees when provided within traditional telephone calling plans.

VoIP does have some limitations. High-quality VoIP calls rely on broadband Internet connections. Therefore, VoIP is not a viable option for users who only have slower dial-up connections. Furthermore, because VoIP uses the Internet to connect calls, VoIP calls can be disconnected if the user's Internet connection goes down for any reason, such as in the event of a power failure—a problem that does not affect traditional telephones, which are not powered by electrical power lines. This is a particularly significant limitation in geographic regions where reliable Internet connections are not yet available. Moreover, any slowdowns or hiccups in the user's Internet connection can cause audible dropouts and other glitches in the call.

The Internet has also led to advances in videoconferencing technology. Videoconferencing allows live audio and video interaction between people located in two or more places. Videoconferencing was first conducted with the use of two televisions connected by a cable. In 1964, the first videoconferencing system was introduced. Although videoconferencing technology continued to develop for many years, it remained largely untapped by consumers and businesses because of its high cost. In 1982, the latest conferencing system cost $250,000 to purchase, with an additional cost of $1,000 per line, per hour, to operate. By the 1990s, advancements in Internet technology and video compression led to the creation of computer-based videoconferencing. IBM's Pic Tel, which was introduced in 1991, was a black-and-white system that cost $20,000 to purchase, with an additional cost of $30 per line, per hour, to operate. Although this represented a significant price reduction, it still kept videoconferencing out of reach of everyone except for governments and large corporations.

In 1992, CU-SeeMe was released for the Apple computer. It was the most advanced videoconferencing system to date. Although it could only transmit video, not audio, its video system was superior to all other systems available for personal computers at the time. Audio was added to the product in 1995. The system, however, was mostly used in classrooms and training facilities because it could only be used to perform videoconferencing among users on the same local network.

In the early 2000s, videoconferencing technology continued to develop with the introduction of widespread, inexpensive, broadband Internet access. During the same time, the price of computers, Webcams, and video capture and display technology declined significantly. In response to such developments, software vendors made improved videoconferencing software, such as Microsoft's NetMeeting and Windows XP Messenger, available. Furthermore, the latest versions of Apple's iPhone and iPad enable their users to make video calls using Apple's FaceTime built-in system, eliminating the need for users to install separate videoconferencing software.

Although telephones capable of transmitting video as well as audio first appeared in the 1920s, they remained too large, complicated, and expensive to become commercially viable until the 1990s. Even then, the relatively high cost of such videophones caused them to be used only by corporations and other large organizations. Relatively soon thereafter, however, the advent of high-speed, low-cost Internet connections made it possible for almost anyone with an Internet connection to engage in videophone calls. This photo shows two employees of a company using Hewlett-Packard's Halo videophone technology to hold a virtual meeting from two physically separate offices. *(Len Vaughn-Lahman/MCT/Landov)*

EXTERNAL COMMUNICATION WITH CUSTOMERS

The introduction of the Internet has made it possible for businesses to engage in more kinds of communication with their customers than ever before. Before the Internet, consumer-focused businesses would advertise their companies and products to consumers using printed materials, such as brochures and advertisements in magazines, and advertisements on radio and television. Almost all companies now provide Web sites to perform many of the same functions as traditional advertising, in addition to many additional functions. Most corporate Web sites include a homepage, a logo, an "about us" section that provides the history of the company, press releases, and biographies or names of company executives, a career search function, terms of use, contact information, and a privacy policy. Corporate Web sites make it easier and less expensive for companies to communicate information to their customers, investors, potential customers, and the press. Similarly, such Web sites make it easier for those who are interested in finding and receiving such information to do so.

In response to the increasing popularity of blogs as tools for personal communication, some companies have created their own blogs for commercial purposes. For example, businesses use blogs to announce new products and events, to receive and answer questions from their customers and potential customers, and to compare their products with those of their competitors. Although such blogs can be an effective way for large companies to reduce the cost of using telephone and print-based communications, they can also be used by small companies to reach a national or international audience that would not be possible without the Internet. For example, "Joel on Software" is a blog by the small business owner of Frog Creek Software. The blog allows company owner Joel Spolsky to provide not only general information about software, but also to promote his particular software business. Without the Internet, Mr. Spolsky would likely not be able to afford to send print mailings to customers and potential customers around the world.

Many companies have taken advantage of the e-commerce capabilities of the Internet. E-commerce refers to the buying and selling of products and services over an electronic system such as the Internet. As Internet usage has increased, so has the emergence of online storefronts, which sell products and services to consumers over the Internet. Such storefronts are sometimes referred to as Web stores, e-shops, virtual stores, and e-tailer Web sites. Although many of the businesses behind these online stores also have physical stores, some companies conduct business solely over the Internet. The largest purely online retailer in the United States is Amazon. Although it was launched in 1995 as an online bookstore, it steadily increased the range of products it offered to include products such as video games, electronics, apparel, DVDs, CDs, food, toys, and computer software. The Amazon Web site lists not only products that Amazon carries and ships directly from its own warehouses, but also products that are sold by other businesses. Amazon lists these products for a fee. Amazon has successfully developed merchant partnerships with stores such as Target, Sears, and Lacoste, who take advantage of Amazon's large customer base and high-quality Web site to generate more sales than they could generate solely using their own Web sites. Part of Amazon's success results from its ability to price many of its products below the retail price of other stores, because it does not incur the overhead costs associated with leasing and maintaining physical storefronts.

To purchase a product from an online store such as Amazon, the customer typically selects the product by clicking a button labeled "Add to Shopping Cart." Once the product is in the cart and the customer has proceeded to checkout, it is necessary to pay for the purchase. Unlike physically shopping in a store, products cannot be purchased online using cash. Instead, payment must be made electronically, using a credit card, debit card, or third-party payment service such as PayPal. Paying in any of these ways requires the user to provide the Web site with sensitive information, such as the user's credit card number. Reputable online retailers take significant efforts to prevent such information from being stolen and used to engage in identity theft. For example, the user's credit card information may be encrypted (scrambled) when transmitted to the online retailer and then deleted by the retailer immediately after the purchase has been completed. If the user's credit card is approved, the Web site typically displays a receipt for the user and sends the order to a warehouse with instructions to ship the order to the user. A carrier such as UPS, FedEx, or the U.S. postal service then ships the product to the customer.

Many online retailers allow customers to provide feedback to other customers about products they have purchased. For example, a customer who has purchased a toaster might give the toaster a rating from one to five stars and write a short description of his opinion of the toaster. Any other users who view the toaster on the same Web site will then see the customer's rating and reviews and any other ratings and reviews of the toaster provided by other users. The Web site might also provide a summary of all of the ratings that have been provided for a particular product, such as by displaying the average rating problems by all users who purchased the product.

(continues on page 70)

Customer Relationship Management

The basis of a successful company is its ability to establish relationships with customers. *Customer relationship management (CRM)* refers to the methodology used by businesses to organize and track customer information for managing customer relationships. Modern companies now use CRM software to collect, store, analyze, and act on customer information as an integral part of their CRM strategies. CRM often involves performing tasks such as helping marketing departments target and develop sales campaigns by collecting and analyzing customer information; analyzing customer trends; distributing campaign material to target groups via e-mail, phone, or postal mail; and analyzing customer requirements using tools such as surveys, focus groups, and interviews. The fundamental goal of CRM is to improve relationships with current customers and build new customer relationships, thereby increasing company revenue and profits.

CRM software collects customer information for use by individuals within a company. For example, CRM software used by an e-commerce Web site, such as Amazon, might gather information about the products purchased by individual customers and demographic information about such customers, such as their ages and zip codes. The e-commerce company may then use CRM software to analyze the customer information so that it can identify dissatisfied customers (such as those who frequently return products) and attempt to improve relations with them, identify highly satisfied customers and attempt to market higher-end products to them, and identify overall trends in product purchases to determine which kinds of products and services to expand and when to perform such expansion. For example, the software might recognize that cardboard boxes have high sales in August (perhaps because college students purchase them before moving into dormitory rooms in September). Either the software or a person at the e-commerce company may respond to this recognition by offering a wider range and larger number of cardboard boxes the following August.

Because multiple departments within a company need access to customer information, CRM systems usually hold customer information in a centralized data bank that can be accessed by multiple people. For instance, when a customer calls the company, the company's CRM software might recognize the identity of the customer based on the customer's phone number and provide the company representative answering the call with immediate access to the customer's purchase history, regardless of which company employee answers the phone. The information provided might include past customer purchases, account balance, product recommendations, and products the customer is likely to buy in the future. Such information might be drawn from multiple departments within the company, such as the sales department, marketing department, and credit department.

As these examples illustrate, CRM is complex. As a result, large companies that use CRM software successfully must integrate several different kinds of software, linking the company's employees among many departments. Failure to perform such integration can result in a CRM system in which individual components work well but fail to achieve the company's goals. For example, consider CRM software that can accurately predict the products that a particular customer is likely to purchase and which contacts the customer to recommend such products but is not linked to the company's credit department. Such software will fail to discover that the customer has a poor credit rating and therefore is unlikely to pay for new products that he purchases. As a result, the company may incur a significant expense in creating and maintaining CRM software that does not increase the company's revenues.

Because of the high cost of implementing a CRM system successfully, many small and midsize companies do not use automated CRM software. Instead, they rely on customer information stored in databases, spreadsheets, word processing documents, and contact management software such as Microsoft Outlook. Company employees then review and analyze the data the old-fashioned way—manually—in an attempt to understand the company's relationships with its customers. Although analyzing customer information in this way can be slow and fail to uncover hidden patterns, it enables the company to retain more personal, human relationships with their customers. The company's customers, instead of receiving an automated e-mail from the company announcing a new product, might receive a personal phone call from an account representative informing them of the new product.

Many companies now use e-mail, whether written by people or generated automatically by CRM software, to communicate with their existing customers and to reach out to potential new customers. Businesses with established cus-

(continues)

(continued)

tomer relationships use automated e-mails with product selections. This is not much different then old-fashioned postal mail sales campaigns that companies send to customers about upcoming sales. This type of marketing is generalized because all customers on the list receive the same mailing regardless of their past purchases. Automated e-mails not only reduce marketing costs for a company because CRM software generates the lead, but a customer receives a list of suggestions based on past purchases. A disadvantage is that automated e-mails carry the risk that the customer will never receive it because their e-mail program places it into the recipient's junk mail file.

The danger in automation is the loss of human interaction between the customer and the customer service representative. Many companies use software to dial a customer phone number and once it is answered a human representative interacts with the customer. While the dialing is automated, because human interaction is necessary to continue the call it will cost a company more money. Some companies have eliminated this cost by using *interactive voice response (IVR)* software that is capable of programming the computer to handle the entire call. Interaction with the computer is two-way—the computer speaks to the customer in a human voice and the customer responds verbally. The computer, however, is only programmed to understand certain words so the interaction can become difficult and frustrating for the customer when the computer does not recognize the response.

(continued from page 67)

These and other kinds of user feedback have turned out to be extremely valuable for online retailers. For example, because Amazon was one of the first online retailers to enable customers to post ratings and reviews, Amazon's database of customer feedback is larger than that of other retailers. As a result, many people research products by going immediately to Amazon to read the customer-written reviews. Once on the site, people are more likely to purchase products from Amazon, even if Amazon does not offer the best selection or the lowest price. In this way, Amazon benefits from the reviews written by its customers.

One advantage of online shopping is that consumers can conduct transactions from the convenience of their homes, offices, or anywhere else. Furthermore, purchases can be made at any time of day or night, on weekends, and even on holidays—online retailers never close. Customers can even purchase some products using the very devices that are used to enjoy those products, as in the case of purchasing and wirelessly downloading electronic books using an Amazon Kindle e-book reader. Furthermore, the Internet makes it possible for consumers to compare features and prices of products with many stores very quickly, without the need to travel from store to store. Price comparison Web sites, such as Price Grabber and Google Product Search, perform such comparisons automatically so that users can search for a product and immediately see a list of the stores that are offering it and the prices at which it is being sold.

Online shopping also has disadvantages and risks. For example, online shopping has led to increased fraud due to the difficulty of verifying the identity of customers when they purchase products from an online store. Despite efforts to protect users' identities using encryption and other techniques, criminals continue to obtain users' private information and to use such information to fraudulently make purchases using stolen credit card numbers. Another disadvantage of online shopping is that it has limited use for products that can only be easily evaluated in person. For example, shoes can be difficult to purchase without trying on. Similarly, online shopping has not proven successful for large or unusually shaped products such as ladders or building materials that are difficult to ship. One common complaint of online shoppers is that returning products by mail can be tedious and time-consuming and that some online retailers have confusing return policies, making it difficult to obtain refunds for returned products.

Despite such problems, one reason that online shopping has become increasingly common is that users can store and access their own account information for each online retailer. For example, the first time a user makes a purchase at a particular online electronics store, the user must provide his or her name, mailing address, shipping address, and other information. Such information is then stored in the user's online account. The next time the user shops at the same store, the user need not enter the same information again. This makes it much easier to make repeat purchases. Similarly, when a user maintains an online account with a utility company (such as a telephone company or an electric company) or a bank or credit card company, the user can view his or her bills and pay those bills directly online. This can result in a significant time savings compared to receiving paper bills and paying them by sending paper checks in the mail. Furthermore, direct online payment reduces the likelihood that payments will be made after the payment deadline. Most companies allow users to pay their bills either by credit or by an electronic transfer from a bank checking account using the automated clearing house (ACH). The ACH is a payment transfer system that all financial institutions are connected to. Its function is to process all electronic fund transfer (EFT) transactions. Before a payment reaches its final destination, it is held until it receives clearance. After clearance the payment is processed and sent to the payment recipient. The ACH is used to process direct payment of consumer bills and for direct deposit of payroll, e-checks, and e-commerce payments.

COMMUNICATION WITH OTHER BUSINESSES

Companies also communicate with a variety of other businesses. This is known as business-to-business (B2B) communication, which involves not only the exchange of information but also the transaction of goods and services between businesses. Businesses communicate with each other for many reasons. Consider a computer manufacturer, which needs to communicate with its suppliers—the companies that provide the components that the manufacturer assembles into a finished product. The company also needs to communicate with its distributers—the companies that transport the manufacturer's products to wholesalers and retailers. Furthermore, the company needs to communicate with businesses that provide it with professional services, such as law firms and accounting firms. These are just a few examples of the kinds of communication that businesses conduct with each other.

Electronic data interchange (EDI) is a technology used for data exchange between businesses via a network, such as the Internet or a VAN (Value Added Network), which is a private network provider that supplies assistance with EDI. EDI arose in the days before the widespread use of the Internet, as a more efficient alternative to communicating compared to more expensive communication by paper or direct human-human interaction. A common example of EDI

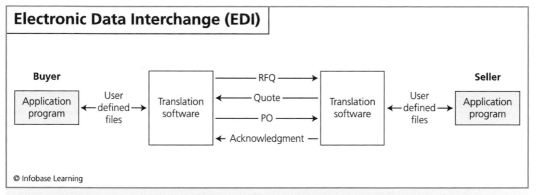

Electronic Data Interchange (EDI)

Buyer

Application program ←User defined→ files Translation software ← RFQ → / ← Quote / PO → / ← Acknowledgment — Translation software ←User defined→ files Application program

Seller

© Infobase Learning

Electronic data interchange (EDI) is a communications standard that enables companies to engage in business transactions with each other electronically over the Internet or other network. This diagram shows an example in which two companies use EDI to enter into a contract purely electronically, eliminating the need to exchange or sign paper documents.

is the interchange between buyer and seller for a purchase order. When a buyer places an order using EDI technology, the buyer's computer transmits an electronic message over a network to the seller's computer. The seller's computer understands how to interpret the information in the electronic order and can process the order automatically. This streamlined approach can save significant amounts of time and money. Estimates show that the cost of processing a paper order can be as high as $70 (taking into account costs such as human labor, printing, and postage), while processing the same order using EDI can cost less than one dollar. Furthermore, while the same order might take up to 10 days to fulfill when transmitted and processed on paper, it might only require one day to process electronically using EDI.

An EDI message is comprised of a string of data elements (known as data segments) that contain one fact, such as information about the price of the product. An EDI message may include data known as a header, followed by one or more data segments, followed by data known as a trailer. The header, data segment(s), and trailer are referred to collectively as the transaction set, that contains information about the product model number, price, billing address, shipping address, and the names of the parties. The EDI message is created by the buyer or seller's computer and transmitted to the other party's computer, where the message can be processed automatically. This computer-to-computer interaction is only interrupted by human intervention when the messages are reviewed for quality, because of error, and in other special situations.

EDI was first created before the existence of the World Wide Web. Early EDI systems therefore used custom EDI software instead of Web browsers and servers. Now, however, EDI can be performed over the Web, making EDI more readily available and easily usable by all businesses. When conducted over the Internet, EDI uses protocols such as file transfer protocol secure (FTPS), hyper text transport protocol secure (HTTPS), and AS2 to ensure secure transmission. This is especially helpful for small businesses because it is no longer necessary for such businesses to purchase, install, and use special EDI software; instead they can use any Web browser to conduct business by EDI.

Web services include a variety of modern technologies that can perform over the World Wide Web many of the same functions as EDI traditionally performed without the Web. Web services technology enables Web-based application-to-application communication between the computers of different companies. Businesses can conduct transactions, communicate with each other, and share data across a network. Web services use the following applications: XML (extensible markup language), SOAP (simple object access protocol), WSDL (web services description language), and UDDI (universal description, discovery and integration). XML is used to tag, or encode, Web documents electronically; SOAP helps transfer data; WSDL provides a description of services; and UDDI lists the available services.

The function of Web services is to enable software applications to communicate with each other directly over a network, so that interaction with human users is not needed. Web services allows, for instance, ordering software to interact with inventory software so that the ordering software can determine whether a particular product is in stock before completing an order requested by a customer. Without the use of Web services, communication between two different pieces of software is often not possible unless both pieces were created by the same company and configured to understand one another. One goal of Web services is to enable such software applications to communicate accurately over the Web even if the software applications were created by different companies and have not communicated with each other in the past. Such interaction can occur because XML tagging allows the definition, transmission, validation, and interpretation of data between each company's applications. SOAP then encodes the

Meg Whitman, Former President and CEO of eBay

Margaret Cushing Whitman was born on August 4, 1956, in the affluent community of Cold Spring Harbor, New York, the youngest of three children of Hendricks and Margaret Whitman. A talented athlete and the captain of her high school's swim team, Meg attended Princeton University planning to become a doctor, but graduated with a degree in economics instead, followed by an MBA from Harvard Business School in 1979. After graduation, she worked at Procter & Gamble in Cincinnati and married Griffith Harsh IV, a neurosurgeon, with whom she has two sons. She then moved to San Francisco to follow her husband's neurosurgical residency, taking a position with Bain & Company and later moving to the Walt Disney Company.

When Massachusetts General Hospital offered her husband the position of chief of neurosurgery, Meg relocated the family to New England, taking a job with

(continues)

Meg Whitman, former CEO of eBay and candidate for governor of California in 2010 *(AP Images)*

(continued)

Stride Rite, a shoemaker, based in Lexington, Massachusetts, where she helped revive the then-struggling Keds brand. Leaving Stride Rite, Meg became the CEO of FTD (Florists Transworld Delivery), a cooperative that she turned into a privately held firm before moving to become the head of Hasbro, where she was in charge of the Playskool and Mr. Potato Head divisions. She was in charge of 600 employees and a division that generated $600 million in annual sales.

Four years after joining Hasbro, Meg was approached by a headhunter with a proposition of joining an online company called Auction Web, a start-up created by Pierre Omidyar, a Silicon Valley computer programmer, who started the firm in order to help his then-girlfriend find other collectors of Pez candy dispensers. Initially, Meg refused to even discuss the possibility of accepting the position, but changed her mind after a meeting with Omidyar. What ultimately influenced Meg's decision was the novel way in which the new company brought people together and provided a functionality that did not exist in the time before the Internet. She was taken by the idea of people being able to connect over shared interests and fascinated by the existence of online communities to which she was introduced by Omidyar. When she joined Auction Web, now known as eBay, in March 1998, the company consisted of 30 people, with a customer base of 500,000 and annual sales of $4.7 million. After a year under her guidance, eBay's customer base increased to more than 7 million users and sales grew to more than $700 million. Over Meg's tenure at eBay, the company transformed into a 15,000-employee behemoth, generating almost $8 billion in revenue with hun-

data before it is sent over the network. In an XML-formatted language, WSDL describes a business's available services and UDDI is a Web directory where businesses list their services and find other service providers.

Companies such as eBay use Web services to help businesses increase revenue and reach new and current customers. The eBay Developers Program offers subscribers a listing manager, customer feedback, and marketing tools to reach consumers. Through eBay API (application programming interface), a business's computer is able to communicate in XML format with eBay's database directly,

dreds of millions of registered users. Despite her success, Meg stepped down as eBay's president and CEO on March 31, 2008, and soon after resigned her position on eBay's board of directors as well as her other board memberships.

In recent years, Meg became involved in politics, helping Mitt Romney, her former boss at Bain & Co. and the governor of Massachusetts, who invited her to join his presidential campaign in the fall of 2006. Meg accepted, becoming one of Romney's finance cochairs and helping raise $12 million in the state of California. After Romney conceded the race and endorsed Senator John McCain for the Republican presidential nomination, Meg cochaired McCain's national campaign, advising on technology and economic issues. Meg was on McCain's list of possible running mates before he chose Alaskan governor Sarah Palin.

In February 2009, after much speculation that her retirement from eBay was a sign that she was about to run for office, Meg announced her plan to run for governor of California, encouraged by Romney, whose father was a businessman-turned-governor of Michigan for six years during the 1960s. Whitman believed that California's budget woes could be solved by running the state as one would a struggling business. She put together a team that included other prominent businesspeople, such as John Chambers, CEO of Cisco, and Scott McNealy, chairman of Sun Microsystems. In May 2009, Meg's candidacy was endorsed by former presidential candidate John McCain. The election was held on November 2, 2010. In spite of spending more of her own money ($144 million) on her candidacy than any other candidate in U.S. history, she lost to Jerry Brown, the Democratic candidate, by 40.9 percent to 53.8 percent.

rather than by logging in to the eBay Web site manually and entering information into a form on a webpage. The benefit for a business is that it can create a custom interface that allows the business to use software to automatically submit items to list for sale, information about a high bidder on an item the business is selling, and the creation of a list of items bid on by the user. The ability to perform these functions more quickly and easily means that the business can spend less time and money on uploading product information to eBay, therefore increasing the profits it earns from each sale.

CONCLUSIONS

Businesses have always been on the cutting edge of developments in communication technology, in large part because businesses are willing to make the investments necessary to design improvements to such technology so that they can improve the efficiency of their communications and obtain the increased profits that result from such increased efficiency. Businesses also have incentives to find creative ways to combine efficient, high-volume, automated communications with personalization so that every customer's needs can be addressed with minimal effort. Modern customer relationship management software, which can automatically send customized marketing e-mail messages to all of a company's customers, is a perfect example of this.

The benefits of such technologies often reach outside the businesses that first develop them, although it may take some time to do so. Customers of businesses that use customer relationship management software arguably benefit from products and services that more closely match the customers' needs and from being notified specifically of such products and services. More significant, as more individuals open small businesses and as even nonbusiness owners seek to market their own skills, to publicize their own blogs, and to communicate with colleagues more generally, the communication technologies that were only available at high cost to businesses just a decade ago are now increasingly available inexpensively online for anyone to use.

4

EDUCATION: THE MODERN CLASSROOM

It is difficult to think of schools without physical classrooms filled with students having printed textbooks on their desks. Some school buildings constructed in the 19th century still have desks with holes for inkwells in them, a relic of the day when students wrote with fountain pens. Increasingly, however, printed books are being replaced with interactive software and physical classrooms are being replaced by, or at least supplemented with, lectures and conversations provided over the Internet to students who attend class from their homes. As with all other technological developments, shifting a lesson from print to electronic form may result not only in a change in the physical media through which information is transmitted, but also a transformation in the process by which knowledge is obtained. This chapter explores a variety of ways in which computers and the Internet are changing the face of education.

FROM TEXTBOOKS TO MULTIMEDIA

Printed textbooks have been used for teaching since the invention of the printing press. *Ars Minor,* a Latin grammar textbook, is believed to be the first book that Johannes Gutenberg printed in 1451. Since the 19th century, standardized textbooks have been the primary means of instruction in primary and secondary classrooms. Teachers rely on textbooks because they are written by experts and tailored for a specific curriculum. Traditional printed textbooks have remained in widespread use because they have multiple advantages. They are low tech, made from materials that are easy to obtain. They are easy to produce, relatively inexpensive to buy, and can be used for several years by different groups of students. Printed textbooks are accessible to everyone and highly portable, allowing students to carry them back and forth between school and home. While early textbooks consisted of text only, advances in printing have allowed illustrations, photographs, and colorful graphics to be added to help capture the attention of students.

Printed textbooks are not without problems. For dynamic subjects like science and history, they can become outdated before they wear out. They can be defaced, lost, or stolen. Since printed textbooks take a one-size-fits-all approach, there can be a mismatch between the contents of the textbooks and the needs of students. A single textbook may not meet the particular needs of different groups of students nationwide or even within a single community, especially since different students may have different learning styles.

Today's students are engaged by audio and video content and may not be as interested in a textbook's two-dimensional text and graphics. For students growing up in a digital world, a textbook's lack of interactivity may engender boredom. Students might even fail to read and absorb assigned material because they are not inspired by static text and images on a page.

Beginning in the 1990s, low-cost personal computers became *multimedia* computers through the addition of color monitors, advanced graphics, CD-ROM drives, additional memory, and CPU power. At the same time, educational content became available in multimedia form. The term *multimedia* refers to content that includes a combination of text, graphics, video, and audio. Early multimedia educational materials were very similar to paper textbooks, except they were in electronic form and included audio and video. They also used *hyperlinks,* which are words or images that can be clicked on to jump to a related page or region of information. Before hyperlinks were widely used on webpages, they were found in multimedia reference works. Hyperlinks allow students to easily look up definitions and explore related topics in a sequence that makes sense to them, rather than in the predetermined sequence picked by the content author. This allows students to cover more ground and to customize the learning experience according to their personal preferences and interests.

Some of the earliest multimedia reference works were multimedia encyclopedias, such as Compton's Interactive Encyclopedia and Microsoft Encarta, which used audio, video, and animation to enhance their descriptions of topics. Although today online encyclopedias can be viewed over the Internet using Web

Hypertext

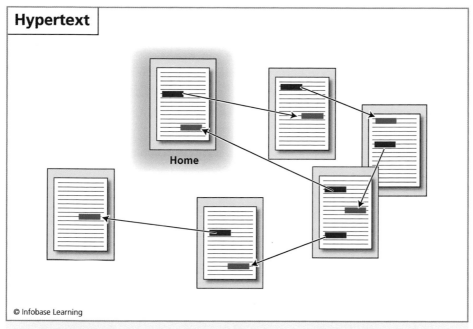

Home

© Infobase Learning

Hypertext documents include both text and links. A link connects one piece of text (the "anchor," shown in red) to another (the "target," shown in blue). The anchor and target may be in the same document or different documents. Activating a hyperlink (such as by clicking on the anchor) causes the target to be displayed. Hypertext is the foundation of the World Wide Web; all Web pages are hypertext documents.

browsers, the first digital encyclopedias were sold on CD-ROMs and therefore had only a limited ability to be updated over time without purchasing a new set of CD-ROMs from the encyclopedia publisher.

One of the key elements of multimedia computer systems is interactivity. Users of multimedia systems can manipulate and control the time, place, and manner in which information is delivered to them. For example, a user of a multimedia encyclopedia can jump from one topic to another using hyperlinks, choose to view a video on one topic, and then choose to listen to an audio clip on a different topic. The user might rotate a 3-D view of the Earth and zoom in on particular content. Many education experts believe that such interactive features of multimedia make it a more effective teaching aid than traditional textbooks because the user is actively engaged with the information being provided, rather than merely being a passive recipient of such information.

Because multimedia educational materials provide information about particular topics in a variety of ways, they provide the opportunity to explain particular topics using the form of media that is best suited to each topic. For example, some concepts are better explained using video media than text, as in the example of cell division presented in an animation of a cell dividing. Other concepts, such as pronunciation of words in a foreign language, are more suited to being presented through audio.

Educators have also pointed out disadvantages of multimedia educational materials. Computers and software are more expensive than paper-based textbooks; students who do not have access to multimedia computers are left out of the loop. Interactive multimedia educational materials can also be more expensive to develop than printed textbooks. Another disadvantage of multimedia systems is that teachers and students must be trained to use the associated computer systems to derive the greatest possible benefit. Traditional textbooks require no such training.

Some educators conclude that spoon-feeding information to students using flashy multimedia materials fails to help the students develop the extended attention spans that are needed to engage in deep thought. Using audio and video can oversimplify abstract concepts and make them appear cartoonish in comparison to carefully worded descriptions. Another criticism of interactive multimedia is that hyperlinks encourage students to aimlessly bounce around from topic to topic instead of focusing on a sequential train of thought in the manner intended by the author. A student can spend hours following hyperlinks and never fully grasp the concept being described.

Although a wide variety of multimedia content is now readily available free of charge on the Internet, such content is often of low quality and has not been required to meet the rigorous standards set by educational standards organizations. As a result, teachers who incorporate free Internet-based multimedia content into their curricula may be failing to provide their students with high-quality content tailored to their specific educational needs.

Teachers and schools who rely heavily on multimedia software for instruction may be removing the human element from the educational process, ignoring the emotional needs of students and depriving them of the support and individual attention a teacher can provide. There are indications that multimedia instructional aids are most effective when used as an enrichment tool, augmenting subject matter that is first taught by a human teacher.

One of the leading makers of multimedia educational aids for elementary school and preschool children is LeapFrog Enterprises. The company was founded in 1995 by Michael Wood, who became interested in using technology to help children learn when he was unable to find products for his own son. LeapFrog's first product was the Leapfrog Phonics Desk, a toy that used integrated circuits to allow children to touch each letter of the alphabet and hear its sound. The Phonics Desk is still in production and now includes an LCD screen that shows a child how each letter is formed. A touch screen capability allows the child to practice writing. Over the years, LeapFrog has offered a variety of educational toys, interactive books, and educational handheld devices. In 1999, the company opened a new division called LeapFrog School in order to provide instructional technology to schools. LeapFrog School develops software and multimedia devices that target school readiness, reading, English language skills, and special education. The LeapDesk Workstation is an example of a multimedia device designed to be used in schools. This device is a successor to the company's earlier Phonics Desk, allowing children to connect letter names, shapes, and sounds using sight, touch, and sound. LeapFrog School also offers the Tag School Reader, a handheld learning tool that interacts with companion books and provides audio feedback and reading assistance.

Although companies such as LeapFrog focus on multimedia devices as instructional aids, others use the resources of the Internet to expand on the role of the traditional textbook. ProjectExplorer, a nonprofit Web site founded in 2003 by Jenny M. Buccos, provides free multimedia educational materials in the form of online travel series. Students can take "virtual field trips" to locations throughout the world. Digital media including text, photos, short videos, and hyperlinks introduce students to a region's language, food, music, and customs. The Web site targets different age groups, from elementary school through high school and beyond. Classrooms, families, and students can learn about Mexico, South Africa, Jordan, and Shakespeare's England.

COMPUTER SIMULATION

A computer *simulator* is a machine or a software application that creates a virtual version of the real world. Simulation can be a useful instructional tool for many occupations, providing a controlled environment that mimics the physical

Simulation and Training Surgeons

Surgical simulators are increasingly being used to train surgeons to perform complex surgical techniques. For example, at the Washington University School of Medicine, a computer-based endoscopic simulator is used to help teach medical students how to guide an endoscopic tube through the interior of a patient's body. At New York Presbyterian Hospital, vascular surgeons who operate on veins and arteries use a simulator to learn minimally invasive techniques that help patients avoid more serious open surgery. At the Oregon Health & Science University School, surgeons use a simulator to practice laparoscopic surgical techniques. These are just a few examples of how simulation is changing the nature of surgical training.

The American College of Surgeons supports the use of surgical simulators as an aid for medical students and physicians who are learning how to perform new procedures or practicing procedures that they perform infrequently. According to a 2002 Yale study published in the *Annals of Surgery,* surgical residents who were trained to perform laparoscopic surgery using virtual reality simulators were more proficient and less likely to make errors in the operating room than residents who were not trained with a simulator. In addition to increased patient safety, one of the main advantages of a surgical simulator over other forms of instruction is that the level of training provided can be customized to fit the requirements and experience of the trainee.

To be effective, surgical simulators must give surgeons the feeling that they are experiencing a real surgical procedure. The instruments used must look and feel like instruments used for real surgeries. Most simulators use a monitor that depicts a virtual reality that includes the tissues and organs of an imaginary patient. The virtual reality that is created by the simulator's software must

world. Simulators are also used in academic settings to help students experience abstract principles, test theories, and develop new skills.

An example of a training simulator that most people are familiar with is a flight simulator, which uses three-dimensional graphics and animation to allow the user to assume the role of a pilot and to control the motion of a plane. Profes-

react to the trainees' actions realistically. When the surgeon-in-training touches an instrument against virtual tissue, the simulator provides tactile feedback that is identical to the feeling of touching real tissue.

A recent breakthrough in surgical technology involves the use of robots for many types of minimally invasive surgeries, including prostate, bladder, kidney, and gynecologic procedures. The da Vinci Surgical System uses a robot controlled by a doctor who is looking through a viewfinder at a magnified image. As the doctor moves surgical instruments in the air, the robot duplicates the doctor's movements within the patient's body. Doctors who use a da Vinci robotic system can train with RoSS, the Robotic Surgical Simulator. The RoSS uses a mock-up of the da Vinci robot and virtual reality to replicate the operation of a da Vinci surgical system. In this case, a simulator of a robot is used to train surgeons to operate a surgical robot.

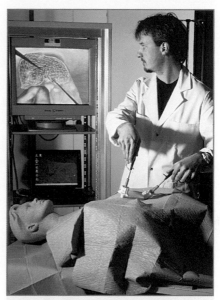

A surgeon is trained to perform surgery using a surgery simulator. The simulator remotely controls the tools held by the surgeon and shows the surgeon a simulated image of what he would see if he were operating on a real person. Surgery simulators can enable surgeons to be trained more safely and inexpensively than using cadavers or live patients.   *(Pascal Goetgheluck/ Photo Researchers, Inc.)*

sional flight simulators that are used to train pilots recreate the environment of a physical cockpit, allowing a pilot-in-training to use life-sized controls. The cockpit may even rotate and vibrate, simulating the physical forces that an aircraft experiences on a real flight. There are also software versions of flight simulators that run on personal computers, the most famous of which is Microsoft Flight

Simulator. Some of these flight simulators are designed as computer games for entertainment purposes only and simplify certain aspects of flight in order to improve the gaming experience.

An example of a computer modeling application that is used in an academic setting is the Stock Market Game, which provides a virtual stock market trading environment. Each student in a class is provided with a virtual investment account containing $100,000. Using information on the Stock Market Game Web site and a live trading simulation, the students must buy and sell stock, attempting to build the best-performing portfolio. In addition to educating students on the intricacies of the real-world stock market, the Stock Market Game can improve critical thinking and help students develop their research and communication skills. Since 1977, more than 10 million students have participated in the Stock Market Game.

Educational Simulations's *Real Lives* is a software simulation that allows students to take on the persona of another person living somewhere else in the world, such as a Brazilian factory worker, a peasant farmer in Bangladesh, or a lawyer in the United States. By experiencing reality this way, students can learn about different cultures, political systems, economies, religions, and geography, as well as about personal issues such as health, family, and jobs. Students can experience the consequences of actions by "turning back the clock" and altering important decisions. *Real Lives* offers first-person simulations of life in 190 countries, using statistical information to create billions of real-life experiences in real time.

Computer simulation and modeling applications can help students gain a better understanding of the world. In addition to learning the facts about a particular subject, students can experience a form of hands-on learning. They can visualize objects and systems that would otherwise be too vast, too abstract, too complex, or even too small to experience directly. For example, a biology textbook might include a formula that explains the rate at which a population of animals grows under certain conditions (e.g., temperature, amount of food, number of predators, etc.). Such a formula sitting on a page may be very difficult to understand, whereas a simulator can be used to show an animation of the size of a population of animals growing and shrinking over time in response to different conditions. The simulator illustrates the real-world meaning of the formula and can be much more effective at conveying its true import.

Simulators and modelers also allow students to ask what if, and then to test various alternatives in a way would not be possible in the real world. For example, students in a physics class might be asked to predict what would happen if an egg were shot with a gun. Different students may develop different theories. Even though it would be too dangerous for students to test their own theories using real eggs and real guns, they could use a physics simulator to test their theories and determine whether they are correct. This enables students to engage in the scientific method by performing experiments even when doing so in the real world would be too complicated, expensive, time-consuming, or dangerous.

Students can also use simulators to develop new skills. Many simulators allow the user to assume a specific role, such as airplane pilot, surgeon, or mayor. Such simulators, if they mimic reality closely enough, can be used to train people to develop the skills necessary to be real pilots, surgeons, and mayors.

Educational simulators help students understand the world by simulating reality quickly, inexpensively, and without risk of harm. Because computer simulations use multimedia techniques to create a virtual world, they can engage the interest of students and keep them interested in a subject in a way that may not be possible with more conventional teaching techniques.

COLLABORATION

The ability to work collaboratively is becoming a critical skill in today's networked global economy. Collaboration has also become an important educational concept. Students who work collaboratively to understand course material or complete group projects become actively engaged in the learning process. Many experts in education believe that students learn more and retain what they learn longer when they work together toward a common goal than when they work in isolation.

Computer-based technology has given teachers and students new ways to communicate and collaborate. When technology is used for collaborative learning, it is employed in three primary areas: instruction, communication, and group projects. Blackboard Inc. is a software company that markets several products for facilitating educational collaboration. One of these products is the Blackboard Learning System, a virtual learning environment and course management system that facilitates collaborative instruction through the creation of online learning modules and entire *online courses*. Another product is the Blackboard Community System, which promotes collaborative communication in an educational community through the creation of academic portal environments. These portal environments connect students, teachers, and school administrations and can be used to communicate information as well as to encourage online interaction between community members.

Another Blackboard Inc. product called the Wimba Collaborative Suite supports collaborative group projects. Familiar interactive technologies including video, voice, and instant messaging are used by the Wimba Collaborative Suite as well as some education-specific technologies such as polling (which allows students to vote on issues and presentations) and whiteboarding (which allows a computer to emulate a classroom whiteboard). Boston University has used the Wimba Collaborative Suite to set up 10 online degree programs. In addition to presenting course lecture material online, the collaborative software allows student mentoring and group projects to be accomplished, with communication taking place via phone, text messages, and live video chats. Professors even offer live online office hours.

Using technology for collaborative learning improves student communication skills. It also develops critical thinking as students evaluate each other's ideas and work through differences in opinion. As students collaborate to complete group projects, they become more confident in their use of technology.

DISTANCE EDUCATION

Distance education is a form of learning in which students are not required to attend a physical school (often referred to as a *brick-and-mortar* school). This form of education has a long history, beginning in 1840 when an English educator named Sir Isaac Pitman (1813–97) offered a shorthand course by mail. This led to the introduction of several types of *correspondence courses* in the mid-19th century in Europe and America. A correspondence course is a course of study that is completed independently at home, with assignments and homework exchanged with an instructor by mail. In their earliest form, these courses helped provide instruction for students who lived in remote locations far from any school. They were also popular among women who would not otherwise have an opportunity to attend school.

Today, correspondence courses that are dependent on the postal service have for the most part been replaced by instruction that relies on the Internet. Technology has greatly expanded the field of distance education, especially in the area of postsecondary education. Online courses and *online degree programs* have become a popular option for many college students. These courses can be less expensive and more flexible than those offered by brick-and-mortar colleges, allowing students to schedule classes around work and family responsibilities. Through online courses, students who are located at a distance from a college or university campus can still enroll. Members of the military use online courses to work toward a degree while still on active duty, rather than waiting until they have left the service to enter a traditional college. In many cases, online education is the only option for students who would not otherwise be able to complete a degree. Although many brick-and-mortar schools also offer online courses as an option, *online universities* such as Concord Law School only offer online courses.

In the 1990s, the field of online education was dominated by for-profit institutions, such as Kaplan University and the University of Phoenix, and targeted older working adults who wanted to finish an undergraduate or graduate degree. In the early days of online education, nonaccredited institutions and *diploma mills* (where students could essentially buy a degree without completing the required coursework) tarnished the image of online education. There was a certain amount of stigma attached to a degree earned through a for-profit online institution.

As a generation of students who grew up with computers came of age in the 2000s, the demand for quality online education grew. Established colleges and universities began to offer online courses, both accredited and nonaccredited. For example, the OpenCourseWare program is a virtual learning environment through which educational institutions freely share educational materials, including course curricula and lecture webcasts. Leading institutions such as MIT, UC Berkeley, and the University of Notre Dame participate in the OpenCourseWare program.

In addition to nonaccredited courses, many colleges and universities (including top universities such as Stanford and Cornell) have established online courses and online degree programs. According to the National Center for Education Statistics, in the 2006–07 academic year 66 percent of public and private colleges offered distance education courses. Nearly 4 million students were enrolled in either a fully online course or a hybrid online/traditional course.

The technology used for online distance education may be synchronous or asynchronous. Synchronous distance education requires the teacher and students in a class to be online at the same time, just as they would be for a class lecture in a brick-and-mortar school. The technology used for synchronous distance education includes Web conferencing, Voice over Internet Protocol (VoIP), videoconferencing, and live streaming. Asynchronous distance education allows students to access lectures and other class materials at times of their choosing. Lectures are viewed via recorded videos and communication takes place through message boards and e-mail. Both types of distance education use e-mail or specialized applications to pass assignments and completed work between teacher and students.

Besides the economic advantages and flexibility of online education, there are other advantages. Some of the more innovative online courses use technology to enhance the materials being presented. For example, Immersive Education is an online education program developed by Aaron Walsh, a Boston College professor and former video game designer. Immersive Education uses virtual worlds to involve students in course subjects, such as allowing biology students to take a trip through the human body or art history majors to fly to the ceiling of the Sistine Chapter to examine Michelangelo's paintings. Other schools are also using virtual reality in online education. At Arizona State University, an Introduction to Parenting course requires students to care for an online virtual child, and at the University of Connecticut students in a homeland security degree program use an urban simulation to learn how to deal with terrorist threats.

The disadvantages of online education should not be overlooked. Critics of online education often mention the lack of face-to-face contact with an instructor. The social life that has long been associated with college is also greatly diminished by distance education. Although many students connect online via chat rooms and e-mail, it is not a replacement for the campus camaraderie and the diverse cultural opportunities available at most brick-and-mortar institutions.

Teachers' unions are mostly opposed to online education, especially at the elementary and secondary school level. There is a fear that increased online education will reduce the number of teaching jobs. Some teachers and professors are also averse to online education since it may reduce their earnings. An educator may be paid for a lecture only once, yet that lecture may be recorded and then broadcast online multiple times to a large number of students over several semesters without providing additional compensation to the educator.

Although some may think that online education sounds like an easier option for students, it can be more challenging. Most online courses allow students to work at their own pace and complete coursework according to their own schedule. This requires discipline and good organizational skills on the part of the student. Access to a computer and Internet connection and familiarity with technology are also required for completion of online coursework.

Many educators believe that online education is the wave of the future and that economic pressures will mean that the expansion of higher education in the United States will take place mostly online. The stigma once associated with an online degree is disappearing as prestigious colleges and universities integrate online degrees, using the same admission standards, faculty, and curricula as their on-campus degree programs. There are also beginning to be more online education programs for elementary and high school students. These programs will surely present a different set of advantages, disadvantages, and challenges than college and university online degree programs.

TESTING

Academic testing in America has its roots in the 19th century, when schools began to test students to determine if they had mastered their schoolwork. Early tests were administered orally or in written form. Over time, written tests came to be the most popular form of testing in schools. They were relatively easy for a teacher to create and could be administered to an entire class of students at once. In contrast, an oral test requires one or more examiners to interview students one at a time.

Several types of written tests became popular in the 19th and 20th centuries. Since a teacher must correct and grade paper tests by hand, some of these new test formats were devised to make the teacher's job a little easier. Multiple choice tests are in this category. Each question in a multiple choice test includes a set of fixed answers for the student to choose from. A True/False test is a form of multiple choice. Besides being easier to correct, multiple choice tests can also be easier to take since they provide the student with a set of possible answers. There are also disadvantages associated with multiple choice tests. They can be harder for a teacher to create and they test only a limited set of knowledge. The questions might be open to interpretation, creating doubt about the correct answer. In the case of True/False tests, it is possible to guess the correct answers without having knowledge of the subject matter.

Other types of tests include matching, where terms are matched with descriptions or definitions, and fill-in-the-blank, which requires a student to supply a missing term within a written statement. Both of these types of tests are easy to create and easy to correct, but they can be more challenging than multiple choice for students who are not prepared.

Students and teachers tend to agree that written essay tests are the most challenging. This type of test requires a written response that fulfills a set of criteria known to the teacher. The test may require a short written response or a longer essay. This type of test is more time-consuming to correct but is often the best way to determine how well a student has learned the class material and how well the student can communicate what has been learned. Students are unable to guess or fake their answers on an essay test, which requires more time to administer as well as more time to correct and grade. Because the teacher or grader judges each essay, there is a certain amount of subjectivity that is not present with other types of tests.

Many mathematical tests fall into a separate category. Rather than just solving problems and supplying answers, they require the student to show the steps used to arrive at the solution. A student may be asked to supply a proof or to apply a series of mathematical rules, all of which must be shown on the test paper. Correcting this type of test can be as time-consuming as an essay test. Like an essay test, it may involve a certain amount of subjectivity on the part of the grader.

The test-taking process in American schools changed little for most of the 20th century. An exam for a particular class was given at a prescheduled time and all students had to attend. The exam lasted for a fixed amount of time and all students turned in their papers at the end. Students were usually allowed to bring only a pen or pencil to the test, except in the case of open book tests, for which students were allowed to reference textbooks during the test. After the test

Distance Education

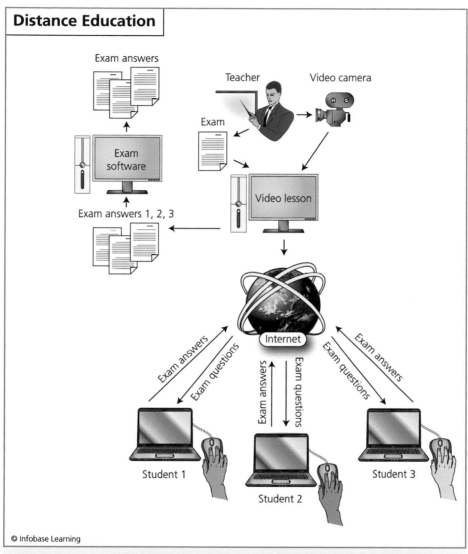

Exam answers

Teacher

Video camera

Exam software

Exam

Video lesson

Exam answers 1, 2, 3

Internet

Exam answers

Exam questions

Exam answers

Exam questions

Exam answers

Exam questions

Student 1

Student 2

Student 3

Distance-education technology enables teachers to teach students without requiring the teacher and students to be in the same physical classroom. Instead, the teacher might be located in a classroom with a video camera connected to the Internet, while each student sits in front of a computer at home. This diagram illustrates an example in which the teacher provides an exam to the students electronically over the Internet. The exam questions are provided to each of the students' computers. Each student submits his or her own answers by computer over the Internet. The answers are delivered automatically back to the teacher's exam software. The students' exams may then be graded either by the teacher or automatically by the exam software.

was completed, a teacher or teaching assistant corrected, graded, and recorded the tests by hand. Students were provided with corrected tests and their grades several days or weeks later. In the case of professional exams, such as a medical or legal licensing exam, the wait for test results could be several months.

In the past decade, the desire to standardize and automate the testing process has led many schools and school districts to institute computer-based testing (CBT). This type of testing uses computers or other electronic devices for student assessment. CBT systems allow teachers to create, schedule, and administer tests. These systems may be stand-alone computer applications, part of a virtual learning environment, or hosted on the Internet.

Unlike traditional paper testing that requires a fixed time and place for testing, a CBT is more flexible, allowing a test to be administered at any time and in almost any location. The turnaround time for a CBT is much faster. Since test evaluation and grading is completed by computer, the results are usually available a very short time after the test is completed. CBT exams are typically limited to True/False and multiple-choice formats. They may be of the open book variety, allowing the student to access reference materials that may be available online.

The differences between paper tests and CBT include different sets of advantages and disadvantages. Before taking a traditional paper test, most students studied intensely. This helped develop concentration skills and provided experience in performing under pressure. However, since paper tests are labor-intensive, many teachers rely on only one or two exams to determine a student's overall grade for a course. Students who are not feeling well or have a legitimate excuse for being ill-prepared on the day of the exam are often graded poorly. If retaking an exam is allowed, a student may have to wait several days or weeks to reschedule. Finally, students often experience additional stress waiting for the results of a paper exam.

With CBT, the speed and low cost of grading benefit both school and student. Knowing the results of a test a short time after taking it (or in some cases, immediately after taking it) means that test-takers no longer spend weeks biting their fingernails waiting for test results. Students can retake a test in a shorter period of time if necessary. Administrative tasks associated with tests are automated, with test results automatically sent to a school's record-keeping system. Some CBT systems perform analysis of test results and provide reports on subject areas that need more instruction. CBT takes much of the drudgery and sub-

(continues on page 98)

100111010010101010011001011101101010100101001

John Sperling, Founder of the University of Phoenix, the First For-Profit Adult Education University

Born into a family of poor sharecroppers, John Sperling (1921–) was raised in a clapboard cabin in the Missouri Ozarks by a domineering mother and an abusive father. After his father's death, which Sperling described as one of the bright spots of his childhood, his mother moved the family to Oregon. Eventually diagnosed with dyslexia, Sperling graduated from high school in 1939 being just barely able to read and, as paid work was scarce, joined the merchant marine as a wiper in the engine room of the ship.

It was at sea that Sperling's education began. One of the ship's engineers befriended him and taught him to read using books borrowed from his shipmates.

After two years, Sperling left the merchant marines and settled in San Francisco. During World War II, Sperling did a stint in the U.S. Army Air Corps but did not see overseas action. After the war, he left San Francisco and enrolled at Reed College in Oregon on the GI Bill and went on to attend graduate school at the University of California, Berkeley, where he was awarded an Ehrman Fellowship to study at King's College Cambridge. He earned his doctorate in 18th-century mercantile history in 1955.

John Sperling, founder of the University of Phoenix, an online university *(University of Phoenix)*

(continues)

100111010010101010011001011101101010100101001

00110101001010011101011010101010101100101010001

(continued)

In 1960, Sperling accepted a tenured position at San Jose State University in California as a humanities professor. He quickly became known as a rebel, organizing a monthlong teachers' strike that culminated with a sit-in at the president's office in 1968.

Sperling's life changed in 1972, when he was picked to run a federally funded series of classes taught by a group of teachers and police officers that were meant to lower juvenile delinquency rates. Sperling implemented a learning system that divided students into small classes and had them work collectively to tackle specific problems. The group-learning experience so inspired the students that they asked Sperling to devise a program that would enable them to complete their degrees despite busy schedules that prevented them from attending traditional four-year universities.

On the advice of a colleague at Stanford University, Sperling presented his innovative curriculum for working adults to the University of San Francisco after his own San Jose State University passed on the concept. The University of San Francisco took a chance on the innovative concept. Using $26,000 of his personal savings as seed money, Sperling launched the Institute for Professional Development (IPD).

Although he himself was a tenured professor, Sperling rejected tenure in favor of working professionals who were experts in their fields teaching at night what they did for work during the day and leading work-oriented peer-based learning groups instead of traditional lecture courses and humanities classes. His research into this model, as well as its application, was more in keeping with what he felt working adults expected from higher education. This approach was met with skepticism and contempt from many traditional academics and regulators, despite a growing demand for it. The primary regulatory agencies in California refused to accept IPD and threatened to pull the accreditation from any university offering IPD programs.

In 1977, after five years of battling California's academics, Sperling relocated to Phoenix, hoping to find Arizona more receptive to his ideas. The newly renamed University of Phoenix secured state accreditation in 1979 and regional accreditation in a record two years. In 1989, Sperling set out to create an electronic distance education system, the first of its kind to offer complete student services and degree programs online. It took five years, but by the mid-1990s when the Internet boom gave rise to online universities, University of Phoenix's online degree programs became a leader among many newly launched online programs nationwide. Today, University of Phoenix employs a comprehensive student learning system with portals to a variety of unique tools and resources including an extensive e-book collection and electronic library, an online tutoring system for mathematics that includes videos and explanatory presentations, a 24-hour automatic academic writing review system, which can check a paper for plagiarism, as well as interactive tutorials and electronic simulations used as demonstrations of real-life decision-making exercises.

In 1994, Sperling took the University of Phoenix holding company, Apollo Group, Inc., public. Today, Apollo Group's market capitalization is just under $10 billion. Sperling, a lifelong Democrat, had stated that if not for his age, he would pursue a career in politics. He supports many liberal causes, providing financial backing for projects that rarely earn him public approval. Together with George Soros and Peter Lewis, Sperling launched an alliance aimed at undermining the so-called War on Drugs, which they decried for its focus on criminalization, as opposed to treatment, and its total dismissal of the possible health benefits of some prohibited drugs. Together, the trio sponsored and passed citizen-backed initiatives in 17 states focusing on treatment and education as opposed to jail time for nonviolent offenders. They also campaigned for the decriminalization of marijuana, especially for medical purposes.

On the scientific front, Sperling became interested in biotechnology, forming a holding company called Exeter Life Sciences. Exeter operates Kronos Optimal Health Company, a preventative health clinic in Scottsdale, Arizona, that creates personalized drug, exercise, and dietary plans for clients with a goal of extending the quality of their lives. Exeter is also the parent company of Kronos Longevity Research Institute, which performs basic and clinical research and develops new assays and clinical reference laboratory services. Serving the scientific and medical communities at large, it also supports Kronos Optimal Health Company's programs and services. Exeter also operates Arcadia Biosciences, a biotechnology agricultural firm that supports research into crop nitrogen efficiency and salt tolerance, which hold the promise of reducing toxic fertilizer run-offs as well as bringing millions of acres of land back into useful farmland production.

Sperling is committed to environmental research to promote sustainable practices and renewable sources of energy and has current projects in the works, including University of Phoenix support of solar research collaboration with other major universities. He has championed major solar initiatives in the states of California and Arizona and started Southwest Solar Technologies, Inc., which is developing unique solar technologies.

(continued from page 94)
jectivity associated with testing out of the hands of teachers, leaving them more time to teach and mentor students. It also allows school districts to administer standardized tests that can be used to assess the performance of schools and teachers as well as students.

CONCLUSIONS

Although education remained relatively unaffected by computer technology for a long period of time, once it began to incorporate computers and the Internet it did so rapidly and wholeheartedly. Many adults today would not recognize the classrooms in which their children are being educated. Even many doctors, lawyers, engineers, and other professionals now find that the skills they spent years developing in school are no longer being taught to the next generation of students. For example, one way the law changes is when courts overrule earlier decisions. Therefore, as recently as the 1990s, law students were taught that whenever they read a court decision, it was necessary to perform additional research, usually in printed books, to determine whether that court decision had subsequently been overruled. Shepard's Citations was a citator, a list dedicated solely to listing court decisions that had overruled previous decisions. The act of determining whether a case had been overruled by looking it up in Shepard's Citations became known as shepardizing the case. Today's law students no longer need to learn this skill because when they look up a case using an online service such as Lexis or Westlaw, up-to-date information about whether the case has been overruled is provided automatically by the online service. This is just one of many examples of skills that have not merely been transformed but rendered unnecessary by the incorporation of computer technology into legal practice.

The challenge for both educators and students is not to allow such advances in technology to serve as crutches. Although it may now be possible to write a paper on nearly any topic in minutes by doing a search on Google and then cutting and pasting from the results, the process of creating such a document teaches its author little, if anything. Educational technology that frees students from the need to manually perform tedious tasks has the potential to enable students to focus their time instead on honing their skills at developing rigorous and convincing legal arguments. If, however, teachers do not push their students to make the most of the time they gain from labor-saving technology and if students do not drive themselves to use the technology at their disposal to surpass the accomplishments of earlier generations who were not fortunate enough to benefit from such technology, then the introduction of computers into education may turn out to be a net loss rather than a net gain.

5

PUBLISHING AND JOURNALISM: THE PRINTING PRESS GOES ONLINE

The publishing industry is so closely associated with words printed on paper that the terms used to describe publications are tied to the printed page and the technology that is used for printing:

- freedom of the press refers to the printing press as the device that is used to create copies of newspapers;
- print media refers to the physical pages on which books, newspapers, and magazines are printed, to distinguish them from broadcast media, such as radio and television, which are transmitted over the airwaves;
- newspaper refers to news that is printed on paper.

Such close associations between particular kinds of written works and the physical means through which such works are distributed were accurate until relatively recently. Now, however, the press provides news not only using printing presses, but also using Web sites, blogs, and Twitter feeds. Books are sold and downloaded online and then read on a computer monitor or e-book reader, without ever spilling a drop of ink. Newspapers are delivered to readers on their computers, without the need for a paperboy or smudged fingers. This chapter explores some of the ways in which computers and the Internet are transforming the publishing and journalism industries and details how these industries are adapting to rapidly evolving technology and business models.

THE PRINTING PRESS

The printing process evolved between the fourth and seventh centuries in Asia, where carved wooden blocks were used to create printed patterns on cloth. This early form of printing was known as *block printing,* in which text and images were carved into a wooden block that was then covered with ink and applied to a piece of cloth or paper. In Korea in 750 C.E., the first known printed document was created using block printing on paper. In 768 C.E., the empress of Japan commissioned a Buddhist prayer to be block printed and distributed. The project is believed to have taken six years to complete and resulted in a million copies for distribution. Many of these copies still exist.

Printing was slower to develop in the West. During the Middle Ages in Europe, hand-copied books were created from vellum or parchment pages that were made from animal skins. The labor-intensive work of copying the book's text was often completed by monks who added elaborate illustrations to each page. These are called *illuminated manuscripts* because of the gold, silver, and brilliant colors that were used for the illustrations. The time and labor involved in producing these manuscripts meant that book ownership was a privilege reserved for the clergy and wealthy patrons who paid to have manuscripts created. The Book of Kells, which is believed to have been produced in a monastery in Scotland in the early eighth century C.E., is one of the most beautiful of the surviving illuminated manuscripts. The gospels of the New Testament are written and illustrated on more than 600 pages of calfskin vellum.

In the 13th century, printed paper from China made its way to Europe in the form of playing cards and paper money. Like other Asian countries, the Chinese had been using block printing for centuries to reproduce both text and illustrations. Europeans recognized that block printing was an improvement over hand-lettered manuscripts. Although block printing is also a labor-intensive form of printing because a block must be hand carved, a single block can be used to make multiple copies. Europeans began to use the block printing process to create prayer cards and other small printed items.

A more advanced printing technique known as *movable type* had been unsuccessfully tried in China. With movable type, pieces representing individual characters or letters (known as *type*) are arranged in the correct order on a block. Ink is then applied to the type to print one or more pages. After the desired number of copies is printed, the pieces of type can be reused and rearranged to print a different page. In China, the extensive number of characters in the alphabet and the use of fragile pottery to create pieces of type limited the use of movable type.

In Europe, the Renaissance saw an increase in literacy beyond the nobility and clergy. There was a demand for written materials by governments and businesses, as well as for educational texts. Several printers began experimenting with movable type. A German printer named Johannes Gutenberg (ca. 1398–1468) was the first to perfect its use. His movable type, which was made from a metal alloy, was durable enough to withstand the printing process. In 1455, Gutenberg's movable type and a *printing press* (a mechanical device that applies pressure to transfer inked type to paper) were used to create 200 copies of a two-volume bible, now known as the Gutenberg Bible.

The use of Gutenberg's printing press and movable type spread rapidly. As the 16th century dawned, hundreds of printers had established businesses across Europe. Scholars estimate that between 8 million and 15 million books had been printed by 1500 C.E. Considering that only a few decades earlier the only books in Europe were handwritten manuscripts in the libraries of the elite, the growth in the number of available books is astounding.

Gutenberg's printing technology played a critical role in increasing literacy during the Renaissance and in the growth of literary and scientific writing during that period. The printing press was the beginning of an information revolution that some argue was even greater in magnitude than the revolution initiated by computers and the Internet. The type of mass communication that the printing press introduced had a permanent impact on the structure of society.

For several hundred years, the movable type printing press was used with very few changes. In the 19th century, the steam-powered rotary press replaced the hand-operated printing press. By then movable type printing had become the predominant printing method throughout the world. Early steam-powered rotary press printers were capable of printing more than 1,000 pages per hour and could print on both sides of a page at once. These innovations brought printing into the Industrial Age.

The next major development in printing took place in 1903, when an American inventor named Ira Washington Rubel developed the offset printing press. *Offset printing* transfers an image from a plate to a rubber blanket and then to paper. By the 1950s, offset printing had become the dominant form of commercial printing and remains so today. Due to the cost, quality, and efficiency

Gutenberg Printing Press

Johannes Gutenberg was born in the German city of Mainz. Although the exact year of his birth is not known, historians typically place it at 1398. His father was a merchant who was a member of Germany's upper class and Gutenberg was a goldsmith by trade. There are indications that Gutenberg was familiar with the block printing process, also known as xylography. His background in metalworking led him to experiment with the use of typography, which uses pieces of movable type for printing.

After moving from Mainz to Strasbourg in 1430, Gutenberg began to create print type from a metal alloy. Gutenberg recognized that once a mold was created, metal type could be reproduced much more quickly than type made from carved

(continues)

This steel engraving imagines Johannes Gutenberg, inventor of the movable type printing press, admiring the first sheet printed by his invention.   *(Library of Congress)*

0011010100101001110101101010101011001010000

(continued)

wood. In 1448, Gutenberg returned to Mainz and obtained a loan from a financier named Johann Fust to set up a print shop. He then built a wooden printing press. This device was based on an existing machine known as a screw press that was used to produce olive oil, wine, and paper. Operation of a lever caused the press to apply constant pressure to inked type so that the ink was evenly transferred to paper. By 1450, Gutenberg had combined his wooden printing press with metal movable type and was printing a variety of texts. It is believed that one of his early printing projects was a Latin grammar textbook called *Ars Minor.*

In 1452, Gutenberg obtained an additional loan from Fust in order to fund an ambitious project—the printing of a two-volume Bible. The project was completed over a period of three years, most likely using multiple printing presses working simultaneously. In 1455, 200 copies of the Gutenberg Bible, known to scholars as the 42-Line Bible (so named because there were 42 lines of text per page), were sold at the Frankfurt Book Fair.

Gutenberg's printing press did not bring him fame or fortune. In 1455, he was sued by Johann Fust, the man who had twice loaned him money, for misuse of funds. A German court turned over control of Gutenberg's print shop and presses to Fust, along with copies of the Bible. Gutenberg was bankrupt, but he is believed to have later opened another print shop. However, his name does not appear on any printed works so it is difficult for historians to gauge his output. When Gutenberg died in 1468, the enormity of his contribution to printing was still unknown. The church cemetery where he was buried was subsequently destroyed and the site of his grave is now unknown. There are no surviving images of Gutenberg. When he began to receive recognition after his death, imaginary depictions of his appearance were created.

Gutenberg's monumental contribution to printing has more than one component. His use of a press was a significant development in the mechanization of printing, allowing pressure to be applied rapidly to a page. Gutenberg discovered the metal alloy that made movable type possible. He also conceived of the idea of molds that could be used to easily reproduce pieces of metal type. Gutenberg's innovations led to the mass production of printed works, putting books into the hands of a large segment of the population who previously did not have access to the written word.

0011010100101001110101101010101011001010000

of offset printing, the majority of books, magazines, and newspapers are still produced with an offset printing press.

FROM PRINTING PRESS TO SELF-PUBLISHING

Publishing companies controlled printing for most of the 20th century, producing newspapers, magazines, and books. Publishing was a specialized industry that required specific knowledge and expertise. The steps involved in publishing included acquiring content to publish, designing the layout of the work, printing it, and then marketing and selling it. If an individual wanted to publish a newsletter, magazine, or book, he or she would have to work with a publisher or printing service and absorb the production costs of the printed work.

The introduction of personal computers, word processors, and peripheral printers in the early 1980s was the beginning of a revolution in the world of publishing. Apple's Macintosh computer, introduced in 1984, popularized the concept of a *graphical user interface (GUI)* that allows the user to interact via on-screen graphics and a mouse instead of only a keyboard and text. In 1985, Apple introduced the LaserWriter printer as a companion to the Macintosh computer. The LaserWriter was one of the first laser printers available to personal computer users. It had a built-in PostScript interpreter, which meant it could print text and graphics in a wide variety of formats.

In the same year, new software applications, such as PageMaker, were introduced to simplify the process of using a Macintosh to create publications. Page-Maker, which was developed by the Aldus Corporation, was one of the first applications to use graphics to realistically depict the printed page. Its use of graphics was described as *WYSIWYG* (pronounced "wizzy wig"), which is an acronym for "What You See Is What You Get." Users of PageMaker with access to a LaserWriter could create and print newsletters and booklets, bypassing a professional publishing company. Paul Brainerd (1947–   ), founder of Aldus, is said to have coined the term desktop publishing (DTP) to describe this new small-scale form of publishing.

Although word processing software had existed for several years, it was solely text-based and required the user to enter special combinations of keys to add text formatting. In the early 1980s, many of the features that are now taken for granted in today's word processors, such as multiple fonts in different sizes, the ability to integrate text and graphics, and support for multiple columns, were only available in expensive high-end desktop publishing software that ran on specialized computers. The Xerox Star workstation, the first computer to combine a GUI, mouse, and laser printer support, sold for $16,000. In comparison, an early Macintosh computer sold for about $2,500. Although this was still expensive for individuals, it was affordable for many businesses, which recognized the value of bringing document layout and publishing in-house.

Early DTP was challenging. The Macintosh had a tiny black-and-white screen with a resolution of 512 × 342 (compared to at least 1280 × 1024 on

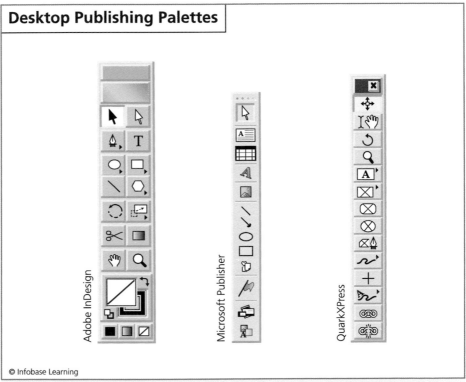

Desktop Publishing Palettes

Adobe InDesign

Microsoft Publisher

QuarkXPress

© Infobase Learning

One way in which desktop publishing software simplifies the process of designing publications is by providing the user with simple tools for performing common tasks. Such tools are often displayed to the user in a palette, which contains icons representing the available tools, such as tools for drawing shapes, copying images, inserting text, and applying hyperlinks. To use a particular tool, the user simply clicks on its icon in the palette, thereby eliminating the need for the user to memorize textual commands. Shown here are palettes from three popular desktop publishing applications: Adobe InDesign, Microsoft Publisher, and QuarkXPress.

1001110100101010100110010111011010100101001

Blogs

Blog is a shortened word for weblog and was coined to describe a type of online journal that consists of dated entries, known as *posts,* listed in reverse chronological order (with newest entries appearing first). The blog concept has been around since the late 1990s, when it was first used by a handful of online diarists. Since then, the blogging community has rapidly expanded to include professional journalists and experts in every field as well as amateur writers who want to express themselves in a public forum. Blogging has become a new form of communication for news, opinion, gossip, professional advice, humor, product reviews, and a wide variety of other topics. It has also become an advertising tool, with corporations hosting their own blogs or paying bloggers to write about their goods and services.

Blogging has several advantages as a form of communication. Blogging has given a platform to amateur writers to provide a wider variety of information and opinions, as well as a fresh outlook. Blogs are uncensored and unfiltered, free from the constraints and agendas that may be applied by traditional publishers of newspapers, magazines, and books. The content of many blogs is covered by a Creative Commons license and can be distributed free of charge, allowing bloggers to share posts.

The proliferation of blogs is also good for the environment. Many organizations that maintain a blog have eliminated the need to send out paper newsletters. Some of the more popular blogs, such as the Huffington Post or the CNN Political Ticker, are credible news sources that for many readers eliminate the need for newspaper and magazine subscriptions.

Blogs also have disadvantages as a form of communication. In *The Cult of the Amateur: How Today's Internet Is Killing Our Culture,* author Andrew Keen argues that the ever-expanding amount of user-generated content on the Internet is destroying professionalism and making it impossible to find quality content by searching the Web. He also describes the impact of amateur content on society as extremely negative, with newspapers and reference works such as encyclopedias being replaced with low-quality, free information.

Another criticism of blogging is that the trend to convert everything to an easily digested sound bite is leading to the demise of in-depth investigative reporting.

(continues)

1001110100101010100110010111011010100101001

001101010010100111010110101010101100101000001

(continued)

Media companies are being driven out of business by nonprofit amateur bloggers, putting professionally trained journalists out of work and lowering the standards of news reporting. Some of the most widely read blogs focus on sensationalism and scandals, as evidenced by the fact that the celebrity gossip blog TMZ is consistently one of the most popular Web sites on the Internet. As blogs replace traditional news outlets, there is a growing threat that real news will be ignored and that the fact-checking professional ethics that are applied to stories by professional journalists will be replaced with rumor-mongering and false reporting.

001101010010100111010110101010101100101000001

today's personal computers). Software frequently crashed and there were often discrepancies between the screen display and printer output. Nevertheless, desktop publishing captured the imagination of a segment of the public who worked through the problems in order to publish original content, eliminating their reliance on a publisher or printing service. Simple DTP projects of the time included business cards, letterhead, and flyers. More complicated projects included catalogs, magazines, newsletters, and booklets.

In 1986, another desktop publishing program named QuarkXPress was introduced by Quark, Inc. It ran on both the Macintosh and on computers that ran Microsoft Windows. It soon became the DTP software of choice for both professional and amateur publishers. QuarkXPress, which is still on the market, supports a variety of layouts for the creation of any type of printed material.

Like Gutenberg's printing press, desktop publishing has led to a revolution in mass communication. Individuals and small organizations can publish content directly without going through a middleman, editor, or censor. DTP has also changed the publishing industry. Many publishing companies now use high-end DTP software internally to create, edit, and lay out their own publications.

ONLINE SELF-PUBLISHING

The previous section described how the technology that enabled desktop publishing affected traditional publishing and printing industries. In addition to self-publishing in print, technology has allowed more people to self-publish online. The Internet has enabled increased communication through Web sites, e-mail newsletters, and electronic magazines and books.

In 1993, an Internet revolution took place when the Mosaic Web browser was developed by students and researchers at the National Center for Supercomputing Applications (NCSA) at the University of Illinois, Urbana-Champaign. The World Wide Web had been introduced a few months earlier. Mosaic made the Web more useful by providing a way to easily access documents. Although it was not the first Web browser, it was the first to support the display of text, graphics, and hyperlinks in an easy-to-use interface. Mosaic, which could be downloaded free of charge, had several million worldwide users within a year of its release.

Mosaic and other Web browsers that followed have had a revolutionary impact on communication. Anyone who was willing to learn *HTML (HyperText Markup Language)* and had access to a computer server that was connected to the World Wide Web could create a Web site. In 1995, a scripting language called JavaScript was introduced to allow dynamic updates of webpages. This meant that a page could be updated based on a user's responses, laying the groundwork for online games and other interactive applications.

Today, self-publishing a Web site is much easier than it was in the early days of Mosaic. Web hosting services rent space on a computer server for a Web site. For simple Web sites, a variety of tools and templates have eliminated the need to learn HTML. For more complex sites, programming services can be purchased online. Many Web hosting companies also provide Web programming for an additional charge.

There are millions of Web sites currently online. Many of these belong to corporations, schools, government agencies, and nonprofit organizations, but a large number are personal Web sites that reflect the interests, opinions, or activities of individuals. There are also Web sites that are maintained by community groups, including youth sport leagues, scouting groups, service clubs, and historical societies. Web sites can also be created for specific events such as class reunions, weddings, and fund-raisers. Information that was previously conveyed through postal mail or phone calls can now be posted on a Web site, where it is available for reference 24 hours per day. Many organizations also use Web sites to recruit new members.

Electronic books are another new form of communication that has been enabled by the Internet. The first electronic books were created in 1971 as part of an effort called Project Gutenberg. Michael Hart (1943–   ), a user of the University of Illinois computer system, decided to launch the project in order to store classic books in digital form. By 1987, Hart had personally typed in 313 books. He then expanded the project and began to recruit volunteers. In 2010, the Project Gutenberg library consisted of 33,000 free electronic books that could be accessed free of charge by the public.

The growth of the Internet in the 1990s made it easier to share electronic books. Project Gutenberg used a simple text format that could be read on any computer, but other electronic book publishers adopted more sophisticated formats. Adobe's Portable Document Format (PDF), which was developed in 1993, was one of the formats used for early electronic books.

The market for electronic books began to grow as more and more books that were in the public domain were transferred to electronic format. Authors who were unsuccessful in finding a print publisher found that they could self-publish online and find an audience. Beginning in 1998, public libraries began to create Web sites that included digital libraries of electronic books. Many of these electronic books were created by scanning printed books and creating digital photocopies. Library users could avoid a trip to their local library or access the resources of a distant library by using the library's Web site.

As the new millennium dawned, electronic books were poised to revolutionize the world of publishing. The growth in electronic books, now known as e-books, will be discussed in more detail later in this chapter.

COMPUTERS AND THE CHANGING NATURE OF JOURNALISM

Since the late 1990s, the prevalence of cable television news programming and the growth of news-reporting Web sites and blogs have thrown the profession of journalism into turmoil. Although the Internet has provided a wider audience for the news and at the same time given more people the opportunity to report on the news and express their opinion about current events, it has also dealt a serious blow to the news business.

Traditionally, most news organizations, whether publishers of newspapers or broadcasters of radio or television news, have earned revenue from the advertisements they provide interspersed with news articles. Although newspapers charge their readers for subscriptions and individual copies, the revenues from such purchases have represented only a small fraction of total revenues. In the case of broadcast radio and television, all revenues are derived from advertising.

Shortly after the advent of the Web, most news publishers created Web sites on which they provided news articles for free. Although they displayed advertisements within such articles, online advertising has not generated nearly as much revenue for news organizations as print and broadcast advertising. One reason for this is that free online news articles often are copied nearly instantly onto other Web sites where they can be viewed by users for free, without ever seeing the advertisements originally displayed by the articles' publishers. Another reason is that the large number of news sources available online means that the same total amount of advertising revenue is divided among a much larger number of competing publishers, resulting in lower revenues for each publisher.

One result of this decline in revenues is that news organizations have become increasingly unable to afford to pay for in-depth investigative journalism. In response to this problem, many newspapers and magazines have experimented with a variety of online business models in an attempt to regrow their revenues and profits. The *Wall Street Journal,* which has the largest circulation of any newspaper in the United States, has always charged an online subscription fee for access to a large portion of its print content. Although most news organizations and commentators criticized this approach in its early years as being contrary to the free and open nature of the Internet, recently several major news organizations, including the *Boston Globe* and the *New York Times,* have returned to this paid subscription model. It is possible that if most or all of the organizations that publish news turn to this model and aggressively enforce infringement of their copyrights, they will be able to return to profitability and be able to begin supporting investigative journalism on a larger scale again.

Ironically, one beacon of hope for the for-profit news industry comes from the nonprofit world of journalism, in the form of the listener-supported news model of National Public Radio (NPR) and other public radio stations. Because broadcast radio is available for anyone with a radio to listen to for free and because funding from government sources is subject to wide fluctuations over time, NPR has always relied heavily on voluntary financial contributions. As a result, NPR engages in massive fund-raising campaigns several times a year in which it urges its listeners to make donations to support its news reporting activities. NPR has developed significant expertise in fund-raising, as demonstrated by its growing body of listeners and relatively strong financial health even in the midst of a significant recession. The approach of NPR is one that may be followed by other news organizations if they fail to develop business models that derive profits from selling advertising, subscriptions, or individual news articles.

THE NEW BOOK

Just a few years ago, most avid book readers would not consider parting with their paper-and-ink books, which could be held comfortably in one hand while at the breakfast table or the beach, in exchange for Adobe PDF documents displayed on a bright computer monitor perched on top of a desk. In the last few years, however, the development of new screen technologies that mimic the appearance of the printed page more closely than ever, and the spread of business models for distributing electronic versions of books to readers easily and at low cost, have begun to make e-books and e-book readers more popular than ever.

Although the three most popular e-book readers on the market today are the Amazon Kindle, the Barnes & Noble Nook, and the Sony Reader, many additional e-book readers are available to consumers. Features shared by many e-book readers, which are enabling them to compete with traditional books for the first time, include the following:

- *Eye-friendly screens.* Viewing text on a traditional computer monitor, whether one incorporating cathode-ray tubes (CRTs) or a liquid crystal displays (LCD), can cause eye fatigue and headaches. The latest e-book readers use special displays that simulate relatively closely the appearance of printed books so that they can be viewed for hours in comfort.

The Amazon Kindle, now in its third generation, is one of the most popular electronic book readers. These devices have gained more acceptance in recent years due to their decreasing size, declining price, improved screen quality, increased battery life, and ability to download electronic books quickly and wirelessly over the Internet. The Kindle and other electronic book readers can display both electronic books and other kinds of documents, such as newspapers, magazines, PDFs, and Microsoft Word documents.   *(Reuters/Landov)*

- *Low power and long battery life.* No one wants to carry a transformer to recharge an e-book reader every few hours. The latest Amazon Kindle can last for up to 30 hours on one charge if wireless networking is turned off.
- *Lightweight.* The latest generation of e-book readers weigh just a few ounces and can fit in a jacket pocket or purse. This makes them as easy to read in bed or to carry on a bus or plane as a paperback book—a significant advantage over laptops.
- *Wireless e-book purchasing and downloading.* It is cumbersome to purchase and download an e-book on a desktop computer and then to transfer it to an e-book reader. Current e-book readers can be used to purchase and wirelessly download e-books directly onto the reader.
- *Notes and highlighting.* Many people who read books enjoy writing in the margins and highlighting text as they read. Today's e-book readers allow such functions to be performed directly within e-books.
- *Reduced cost.* Now that e-book readers can be purchased for $100–$200 and e-books themselves are less expensive than hardcover books, frugal consumers are increasingly turning to e-books as a way to read the latest best sellers at a fraction of the hardcover price.

E-book technology is far from perfect. It can be difficult to quickly scan through multiple pages of an e-book to find a snippet of text or to jump back and forth between different sections of an e-book. Because only one page from one e-book can be viewed at a time, e-books are not particularly well-suited for performing research projects that require reviewing several books simultaneously. Black-and-white e-books do not allow highlighting or taking notes in multiple colors. E-book readers are more susceptible to damage from falls, water, and food than traditional books. Finally, many people prefer the appearance, feel, and even the smell of paper books. Despite all of these drawbacks, the third generation of the Kindle was Amazon's top-selling product in 2010.

Although e-books provide publishers with an additional avenue through which to sell books, many book publishers are finding even a partial shift from printed books to e-books to be challenging. One reason is that e-book vendors

1100111010010101010011001011101101010010101001

Brad Templeton, Electronic Publishing Pioneer

Brad Templeton was born near Toronto, Canada, in 1960 to Charles and Sylvia Templeton and earned a bachelor's degree in mathematics from the University of Waterloo. Templeton encountered his first computer, a mainframe, as a teenager in 1976, thus beginning a lifetime involvement with computers and computer programming. A few years later, Templeton sold a PC game to Personal Software, which became VisiCorp, the first software application company of the personal computer industry. Templeton was hired as Personal Software's first employee, tasked with writing games and other programs. He quickly realized that networking computers together would be much more important for the future of the computer industry and spent a lot of time writing various networking applications, as well as software for both the PC and Macintosh platforms.

(continues)

Brad Templeton, electronic publishing pioneer   *(Joi Ito; licensed under a Creative Commons Attribution license)*

1100111010010101010011001011101101010010101001

Templeton participated in building and developing USENET and, together with Henry Spencer, made USENET's first international link. Templeton was the first to suggest the current Internet address format, user@toplevel-domain, and to separate the subsequent levels with dots (such as email@website.com). He also founded and edited "rec.humor.funny," a moderated newsgroup that collects, archives, filters, and distributes jokes to its subscribers, as well as its Web site, www.netfunny.com, the world's longest-running blog. In 1989, he created the first dot-com business, a company that used the Internet as a platform to deliver services, called ClariNet Communications Corporation. ClariNet sent an electronic newspaper to registered subscribers by gathering information from multiple wire services and organizing it into a constantly updated package delivered to subscribers over the Internet. The subscribers were Internet service providers, who made ClariNet's newspaper available to their clients as a part of their service agreement.

In 1997, ClariNet, together with the ACLU, Electronic Frontier Foundation, and other electronic publishing companies and nonprofit organizations, was a plaintiff in the landmark case of Reno v. ACLU, in which the U.S. Supreme Court held the online censorship provisions of the *Communications Decency Act* (CDA) of 1996 to be unconstitutional. The CDA aimed to protect minors from inappropriate and indecent materials on the Internet by criminalizing "knowing transmission of obscene or indecent messages to any recipient under 18 years of age," as well as sending or displaying a message that may be found "patently offensive." Templeton joined the effort to strike down these provisions, pointing out that some of the jokes published on rec.humor.funny, as well as legitimate news articles, may be found to be offensive because they contain vulgar lan-

such as Amazon have pressured publishers to accept lower prices for e-books than for traditional books. Publishers have argued to Amazon that the cost of producing a book, including the cost of paying an author, artists, editors, and all of the other professionals involved in the publishing process, has not gone down, and that the cost of an e-book should not be significantly lower than that of a printed book, even if some price reduction attributed to the elimination

guage or explicit descriptions of violent acts of rape and murder and could thus be in violation of the CDA, even though they would be within legal bounds if printed in a newspaper or broadcast over cable television. In the affidavit submitted to the court, Templeton stated that upholding the CDA would require him as well as other Internet publishers to assess the risks of running the potentially offensive articles against the benefits of informing the public of the events, effectively forcing them to censor the news they publish. The Court found these provisions of the CDA to be in violation of the First Amendment right to freedom of speech and concluded that Internet speech cannot be regulated in the same way that the Federal Communications Commission regulates television and radio transmissions.

Templeton sold ClariNet to Individual, Inc., in 1997, at which time it had over 1 million readers. He left ClariNet in 1998 when Individual merged with Desktop Data, forming Newsedge Corporation. Since then he has taken on a variety of part-time projects, including providing capital and serving as an adviser to several start-ups. He sits on the board of BitTorrent, Inc., and is chairman of the board of the Electronic Frontier Foundation, an organization protecting privacy and freedoms in cyberspace. Templeton is also on the board of the Foresight Nanotech Institute, a leading advocacy group for molecular nanotechnology founded in 1986. He is currently involved with Caller App Inc., a new start-up that intends to reinvent the phone call.

Templeton published several joke books with material gathered from rec.humor. funny, as well as the CD-ROM *Hugo and Nebula Anthology 1993*. He is also involved in photography and amateur theater and is a popular panoramic artist at the annual Burning Man festival in Nevada. Templeton lives in Silicon Valley, California.

of paper and transportation is justified. Publishers are also finding themselves squeezed by increased competition in the form of self-published books, online encyclopedias, and blogs. Furthermore, publishers, which originally competed only with other publishers in the same region or country, now find themselves competing with publishers everywhere in the world. All of these forces are putting pressure on publishers to operate more efficiently and, as a result, to accept lower profit margins and in many cases lower total profits, which results in a decreased ability to pay authors, editors, sales staff, and everyone else who makes the publication of books possible.

It is still too early in the history of e-books to determine what their final impact will be on the publishing industry. Although traditional publishers, as a whole, have so far suffered more than benefited from the shift to e-books, the total picture is more complex. Book publishers, precisely because of their experience and expertise, can move into electronic publishing on a large scale more quickly than individuals and purely Web-based companies. E-book readers provide traditional publishers with the opportunity to effectively republish books in electronic form that have long been out of print and thereby to obtain new readers for—and generate new profits from—such books. The relationships that book publishers have with established and popular authors enables them to promote e-books more widely and successfully than self-published authors. Astute readers who purchase e-book readers and who seek high-quality works of fiction and nonfiction will likely purchase e-books published by traditional publishing houses rather than online publishers. Although it will likely take some time for business models in the publishing world to adapt to e-book technology, it is quite possible that traditional publishers will emerge stronger than ever.

CONCLUSIONS

The publishing industry is in a state of significant flux, some say revolution, in large part as a result of developments in computer and Internet technology. Newspapers that were in business for more than a century have gone bankrupt, while others scramble to recover lost advertising and subscription revenue. Book publishers face increased competition not only from self-published authors and Web sites, but also from increased use of video games and social networking sites.

At the same time, the more hours people spend using computers, the more time they spend reading and writing. Internet users are voracious readers. This presents an opportunity for publishers to find ways to attract audiences on the Internet as customers.

The Apple iPad is one of many devices that can now be used to subscribe electronically to digital editions of newspapers, magazines, and other publications. Once a user has subscribed to a particular publication, each new edition is transmitted automatically to the iPad or other device over the Internet so that it is ready for the user to read at his or her convenience. Many traditional publishers are turning to electronic subscriptions as a way to recover from some of the decline in subscriptions to their print editions, representing a shift away from providing free content on the Web.   *(UPI/Apple, Inc./Landov)*

Some recent trends provide promise for publishers and for the authors, editors, artists, and others they employ. One is the growth in popularity of low-cost, lightweight, mobile Internet devices, such as the BlackBerry, iPad, and Kindle. Such devices make it possible to provide both readers and publishers with the best of both traditional publishing and online publishing. For example, it is possible to pay for a subscription to a newspaper such as the *New York Times* and to then obtain a daily copy of the newspaper delivered to the user's iPad wirelessly and automatically every day. The form factor of the iPad makes it suitable for reading at a kitchen table or on a train, yet without the hassle of buying a newspaper at a newsstand or disposing of it in a recycling bin. Such devices also typically include protection against copying of such digital media, thereby protecting the publisher against lost sales.

Also promising are some signs of a return to quality among readers who are now actively seeking out content produced by professional publishers after becoming dissatisfied with blogs and other online publications that offer little more than speculation and copying of original content. The rebirth of the publishing industry may very well depend on the taste and good judgment of readers and on the development of similar habits and purchasing decisions of future generations.

6

ACCESSIBILITY: ACCOMMODATING PEOPLE WITH DISABILITIES

As technology plays an ever-expanding role in everyday life, expectations for what it can accomplish are constantly rising. This is particularly true for people with disabilities, to whom technology offers improved access to employment, education, and leisure activities. It can support increased independence at home and in the community and provide a means for communication and civic participation. *Assistive technology* is an umbrella term that includes many types of adaptive and rehabilitative devices for people with disabilities. Computers are increasingly becoming the cornerstone of assistive technologies, but the process of ensuring that computers are useful, accessible tools for any user is still evolving.

Numerous types of impairments, of varying severity, can affect computer use. These include the following:

- Visual impairment, such as low vision, complete or partial blindness, and color blindness.
- Hearing impairment, including deafness or difficulty hearing.
- Motor or dexterity impairment, such as paralysis, cerebral palsy, or carpal tunnel syndrome and repetitive strain injury.
- Cognitive impairments and learning disabilities, such as dyslexia, attention deficit disorder, or autism.

A variety of hardware and software products can facilitate access, interaction, and use of computers at home, work, or school for people with disabilities. Some of these include modified or alternate keyboards, switches activated by pressure, touch screens, voice recognition tools, and visibility enhancements.

INPUT TECHNOLOGY FOR PEOPLE WITH DISABILITIES

Input is what happens whenever a user enters data into a computer. Input can include text typed in a word processing document, keywords entered in a search engine, or data entered into a spreadsheet. Input can be as simple as clicking a mouse button or as complex as scanning a document or downloading photos from a digital camera. Devices such as the keyboard, mouse, scanner, or digital camera are considered input devices. For people with disabilities, alternative devices can facilitate this process in a variety of ways. These devices include alternative keyboard and mouse systems, head-operated pointing devices, switches, touch screens, voice input systems, voice recognition software, dictation software, and ergonomic computer-based equipment. The following sections will describe some of these tools and how they are used.

Speech Recognition Software

There are two uses for speech recognition systems: dictation, or translation of the spoken word into written text, and computer control via spoken command. If configured properly, speech recognition can provide the user a certain amount of hands-free control over the computer. A user can speak, rather than type, a command such as "start Microsoft Word" or "start Internet Explorer." If the user lacks control over upper extremities, then headset/microphone placement becomes a critical consideration.

When users are first introduced to speech-recognition software, they might be surprised at how differently computers and human beings listen to and understand speech. The first challenge in speech recognition is to distinguish between speech and background noise. When a user speaks to a computer, he or she should be in a quiet place and should speak clearly into a properly positioned microphone. A second challenge is recognizing speech from more than one speaker. People naturally adjust to the unique characteristics of every voice. Speech-recognition software, on the other hand, works best when the computer has a chance to adjust to each new speaker. The computer must first be trained, or taught, to recognize a particular user's voice before the computer can accurately recognize that user's speech. Another challenge is distinguishing between words and phrases that sound alike. Common sense and context help human beings decide whether a speaker said "ice cream" or "I scream." Since a computer cannot rely on common sense, speech-recognition programs keep track of how frequently words occur by themselves and in the context of other words. This information helps the computer choose the most likely word or phrase from among several possibilities. Finally, people sometimes mumble, slur their words, or leave words out altogether. Human listeners can usually fill in the gaps. Unfortunately, computers only understand what was actually spoken. One of the most effective ways to make speech recognition work better is to practice speaking clearly and evenly.

Adaptive and Alternative Keyboards

The most common means of using a computer today generally involves a keyboard and mouse. These tools have been adapted in a variety of ways to make them easier for people to use. Most keyboards have embossed locator dots that help any user find the "home" keys, F and J, without looking. Another standard feature is the sticky keys function, which allows users to press a key—such as the shift key—and release it, then press another key without having to press both simultaneously. This feature is particularly helpful to users who have limited use of their fingers and who can only depress one key at a time.

Other modifications include extra-large keys or keys with larger print and high-contrast colors. Adjustable keyboards break into two or three sections that can be positioned close together or further apart or rotated and tilted to many angles. Some highly specialized keyboards have only a few buttons, resembling the fingers of a hand that can move north, south, east, west, and straight down. The user's fingers move less than half an inch in each direction. A *chorded keyboard* allows the user to enter characters or commands by pressing several keys together, like playing a chord on a piano. The large number of combinations available from a small number of keys allows text or commands to be entered with one hand. The most compact versions of this device, called keyers, resemble a bicycle handlebar. Keyless keyboards eliminate the need to press keys at all. One style features two domes where the user's hands rest. Each dome can slide independently into various positions from a central resting point. Another keyless device allows people with limited or no hand movement to access a computer using only slight hand or head motion. The keyboard works with the slightest touch of a wand that can be held in the hand or the mouth.

As for mouse modifications, buttons may be enlarged, shrunk, or simplified to make them more comfortable to use. Scroll wheels remove the need to locate the scrolling interface on the computer screen, and some trackball models can even be operated by foot.

Keyboard and Mouse Alternatives

Some people may be unable to use a conventional input device, such as a keyboard or mouse. Keyboard shortcuts and mouse gestures are one way to achieve this. Other solutions include on-screen keyboards and alternate input devices such as switches, joysticks, touch pads, and trackballs. Some highly specialized hardware and software combinations offer still more alternatives.

One system lets people with physical disabilities operate a computer with their eyes. By looking at control keys displayed on the monitor, a user can synthesize speech, control his environment (such as lights and appliances), type, operate a telephone, run computer software, and access the Internet. A similar tool uses a monitor-mounted camera that focuses on the user's eye. By determining where the user is looking, the software can move the cursor around the screen. Mouse clicks can be prompted by a slow blink, a long glance, or a hardware switch. A head-tracking mouse transmits a signal from atop the computer and tracks a reflector placed on the user's head or eyeglasses. This alternative allows the person control over the movement of the cursor using only the movement of his head. Turning the head to the left directs the cursor to the left. Turning the head to the right moves the cursor in the same direction. This tool only provides control over mouse movements. It does not provide mouse functions such as a click.

Switch Access Scanning

Switch access uses one or more switches to let the user select from an electronic set of graphic images or characters. This is a slow, but functional, alternative for individuals with significant movement limitations. The user needs only to have consistent control of one or more body parts for accessing a single switch or multiple switches. The switches can be controlled by hand or by a head-mounted accessory. One such accessory is called a *sip/puff switch*. A head frame with attached mouth tube and switch box let the user inhale or exhale through the tube to operate the two-way switch. A leaf switch lets the user press a small padded sensor to activate the switch. A TouchFree Switch uses a combination of a digital video camera and switch software that can be activated by large or small body movements.

Renowned astrophysicist Stephen Hawking is perhaps the most visible user of this type of assistive technology. At age 21, he was diagnosed with amyotrophic lateral sclerosis (ALS), a disease of the nerve cells in the brain and spinal cord that control voluntary muscle movement. Dr. Hawking requires assistance for most movement and is unable to speak. He has used a thumb switch and a blink-switch attached to his glasses to control his computer. By squeezing his cheek muscles and blinking, he activates an infrared switch that allows him to scan and select characters on the screen to compose speeches, surf the Internet, send e-mail, and "speak" via voice synthesizer. With these tools, he has been able to research and write many books, including *A Brief History of Time, The Theory of Everything,* and *On the Shoulders of Giants.*

OUTPUT TECHNOLOGY FOR PEOPLE WITH DISABILITIES

Output refers to the text, images, sounds, and printouts produced by computers. Assistive output technology such as Braille display and output devices, Braille embossers and printers, screen reading software, and screen magnification software enable blind and vision-impaired people to use or interact with computers. A screen reader application reads aloud information displayed on a computer monitor screen, both text within documents and information in dialog boxes. Screen readers also make menu selections audible. Screen magnification software enlarges the viewing area of a computer monitor display. Some software applications combine screen magnification, a screen reader, and a text reader. Finally, there are applications that use a flatbed scanner with optical character recognition software to transfer printed pages to the computer and magnify them, print them in Braille, or read them aloud.

Text reader, or *text-to-speech,* applications should not be confused with *screen readers.* Text readers primarily read aloud text as it is keyboarded or read

A blind computer user uses a Combibraille device to read text output by a computer. The device converts text from the computer into Braille characters that the computer user can read using her fingertips.   *(© Michael Newman/PhotoEdit)*

aloud text within digital documents such as e-mails or word processing documents. These software applications are more likely to be used by people with learning disabilities, people with poor reading abilities, or speakers of English as a second language.

The Problem with Cell Phones

Cell phones have revolutionized life for most people, but for people with vision loss, finding a cell phone that they can use is nearly impossible. For example, features such as keys that can be identified by touch, displays that can be read by people with limited vision, and phones with speech output for those who cannot read the phone's display are not widely available. Section 255 of the Telecommunications Act of 1996 requires cell phones and phone services to be designed to be accessible for people with disabilities, but this technology has yet to catch up with users' needs. A limited selection of off-the-shelf phones offers adapted access to some—but not all—cell phone features. Some phones are compatible with third-party *screen reader* programs that provide speech output to support nearly every feature and function on a phone. One phone, the Owasys 22c, was designed specifically for people who are blind or severely visually impaired. It has no screen, highly tactile buttons, and provides speech output access to many features. However, it doesn't play music, read e-mail, or surf the Web.

Developing Technology

One area that holds promise for visually impaired computer and mobile phone users is the field of *haptic technology.* The term *haptic* comes from the Greek *haptesthai,* meaning "to touch." Scientists have studied haptics for decades, and they know quite a bit about the biology of touch. Unfortunately, visual and auditory cues are easy to replicate in computer-generated models, but tactile cues are more problematic. In 1993, the Artificial Intelligence Laboratory at MIT constructed a device that delivered haptic stimulation, finally making it possible to touch and feel a computer-generated object. Today, it is not difficult to think of potential applications such as the following:

- Video game makers have been early adopters, taking advantage of vibrating joysticks, controllers, and steering wheels to reinforce on-screen activity. Some touch screen manufacturers are experimenting with this technology as well.
- Nokia phone designers have perfected a tactile touch screen that makes on-screen buttons behave as if they were real buttons. When a user presses the button, he activates two small sensor pads under the screen, which is designed to move slightly when pressed. Movement and sound are synchronized perfectly to simulate real button manipulation.
- Computer scientists are experimenting with using haptic technology to create touchable maps for the blind. Researchers shoot video of a real-world locale or building, then software evaluates the video frame by frame to determine the shape and location of each object. The data results in a three-dimensional grid of force fields for each structure. Using a haptic interface device, a blind person can feel these forces and, along with audio cues, get a much clearer idea of a city or building's layout.

Accessibility Issues

Accessible computing is a field that seeks to make computer systems accessible to all users, regardless of disability or severity of impairment. It includes software applications adapted for people with disabilities, operating system accessibility options, and accessible Web browsers. Web sites can be made more accessible if they conform to accessible design principles. For instance, the tendency to indicate meaning using methods that are purely visual—such as font size, color, or images—restricts access to some users.

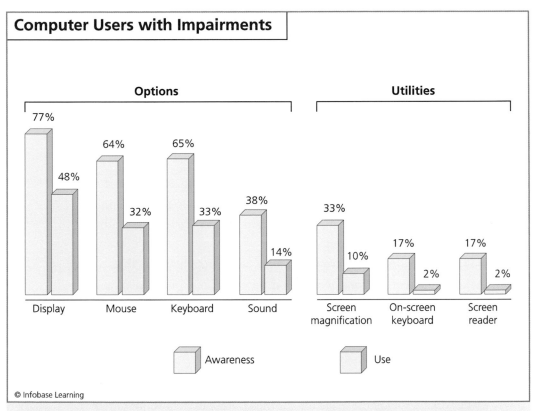

Computer Users with Impairments

Those who design computers, peripherals (such as monitors, keyboards, and mice), and software have developed a wide variety of technology for assisting those with impairments to made productive use of computers. This chart, based on a study conducted by Forrester Research and commissioned by Microsoft, shows how frequently users with mild or severe impairments are aware of and make use of computer accessibility options and utilities. As the chart illustrates, users with impairments make much more frequent use of accessibility options built in to existing computer hardware and software (such as options for increasing the font size displayed on a monitor) than separate accessibility utilities, such as screen magnifiers.

1100111010010101010100110010111011010100101001

Assistive Technology Success Stories

Many lives have been changed dramatically by assistive technology. The right tools can make communication possible, open career doors, and help people with physical impairments reach their fullest potential. Some of those success stories follow.

Sangyun Hahn is a computer scientist who has been blind since the age of six. He attended a school for the blind from elementary to high school, as most blind children do in his native Korea. When he became an undergraduate in a large university full of sighted students, it was a big change. Classrooms were hard to find. The university lacked a support system for the blind, so he recruited volunteers to read books to him. He began to learn about computers in his first year and used a simple screen reader and word processor program. OCR technology was another breakthrough, because he could scan a book, translate the text into Braille, emboss it, and read it. He was fascinated by the technology and began learning a programming language so he could write a program to clean up and format scanned text for Braille translation. Several computer science classes followed, and Hahn eventually applied and was accepted to the computer science department at his university. After graduate school, he came to the United States to pursue his doctorate at the University of Washington. Several new technologies helped with his studies there, such as a Braille note taker that allowed him to write Braille documents, read computer files downloaded from a PC, and translate Braille documents into printed non-Braille text. It also contained a Web browser, e-mail client, calculator, schedule organizer, and audio recorder. Han's research focuses on tactile graphics.

Paul Filpus was a 29-year-old civil engineer working in the construction industry when he lost his eyesight in a car accident. He completed a rehabilitation program, followed by a six-month term at a business college. His studies in data processing led to a 31-year career as a computer programmer-analyst. He retired in 2003. Filpus has experienced amazing technological strides during his lifetime. "A Perkins Brailler and a cassette recorder were important tools for me, both at the computer school and throughout my time at work," he said. "My employer purchased all the necessary adaptive devices and software tools that I needed over the years to access electronic and print information. Braille output was provided right from the beginning, but the main tool in the later years of my career was a

(continues)

1100111010010101010100110010111011010100101001

(continued)

personal computer with speech access." He wrote and tested computer programs for a business applications programming group and also worked for a medical instrument research and development group. "Comparing the computer hardware and software of today to what it was when I entered the field 31 years ago would be like comparing today's society with that of ancient times," he said. "I would think most blind students of today would have opportunities to get experience in using personal computers with a number of software packages while still in high school. Getting further education in college could then lead to career positions."

Adrian, an elementary school student in Oakland, California, cannot walk, speak, or use any of his limbs. But the 11-year-old can control the movement of his eyebrows, and so, amazingly, he can communicate. His teacher and other specialists spent three years trying to locate a place on Adrian's body that would allow him to communicate using a sensor and switch. Adrian wears a headband that can sense the movement of his eyebrows. That motion triggers the computer cursor to move to a row or column on the monitor that illustrates what he's trying to express, and the computer then utters the words he has chosen. This particular computer has pictures tailored especially for Adrian: photographs or pictures of friends and family, including his baby sister, Alexis, and pictures or words depicting situations or events he would like to write about, such as the weather, trips with family, and meal preferences.

Lukas, a high school sophomore in Spokane, Washington, has extremely limited use of his arms and legs as a result of a birth defect. But that hasn't kept him from playing a musical instrument. When he brought home a note seeking permission to play a band instrument, his mother signed it and said, "Lukas, just go and see what's going to work." He chose a euphonium, a type of tuba. At first, Lukas just blew into the euphonium without using the finger valves, but that meant he could play only one note. Although he patiently waited until that note showed up in a musical score and seemed happy to do just that, his upbeat attitude paid off. A school employee sought out a music-store owner who was also a musical-instrument inventor and repairman. The inventor designed a euphonium with a joystick that electronically signals the valves of the euphonium to move. Later, an engineer helped refine the joystick technology. Lukas may have some mechanical help with his instrument, but his personality has turned his desire to make music into a reality.

In 1998, Congress amended the Rehabilitation Act of 1973 to require federal agencies to make electronic and information technology accessible to people with disabilities. The amended law, commonly known as Section 508, was enacted to eliminate barriers in information technology, open new opportunities for people with disabilities, and encourage development of technologies that will help achieve these goals. The law applies to all federal agencies when they develop, procure, maintain, or use electronic and information technology. It includes Web sites and other online publications. Under Section 508, agencies must give disabled employees and members of the public access to information that is comparable to the access available to others.

ERGONOMICS

Ergonomics is the science of fitting workplace conditions and job demands to the capabilities of the working population. A successful fit can promote productivity, lower the risk of injury, and increase workforce morale. According to the U.S. Department of Labor, Occupational Safety and Health Administration (OSHA), repetitive strain injuries are the nation's most common and costly occupational health problem, affecting hundreds of thousands of American workers and costing more than $20 billion a year in worker compensation. Low-tech assistive devices can reduce the likelihood of repetitive stress injuries, operator fatigue, and discomfort. These tools include adjustable workstations, adapted furniture, writing aids, modified seating and lighting, and wrist and back supports. In addition to the adaptive technology mentioned earlier in the chapter, ergonomic changes to a computer workstation might include simply adjusting the position of your computer keyboard or making sure that the height of the desk chair allows your feet to rest flat on the floor. The average person should have the top of their monitor at or just below eye level. Elbows should be close to the body and supported, and wrists and hands should be in line with forearms.

Universal design is the practice of creating products and environments that are usable by all people, to the greatest extent possible, without adaptation or specialized design. This user-friendly approach is concerned with comfort and ease for all, not just those with special needs. For example, everyone benefits from a stepless entryway, whether using a wheelchair, pushing a stroller, or carrying groceries. Wider doorways in public buildings offer better wheelchair access, but also make navigation easier for everyone who passes through them.

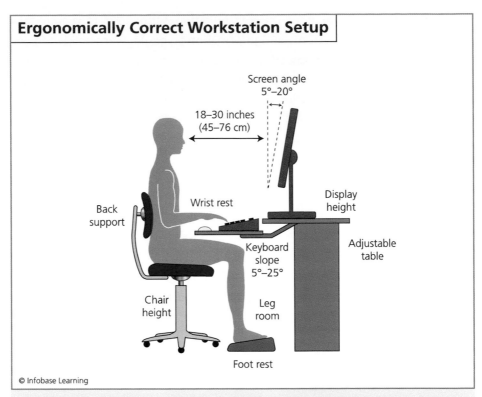

Ergonomically Correct Workstation Setup

Screen angle
5°–20°

18–30 inches
(45–76 cm)

Display
height

Back
support

Wrist rest

Keyboard
slope
5°–25°

Adjustable
table

Chair
height

Leg
room

Foot rest

© Infobase Learning

Someone who uses a computer without an ergonomically correct configuration of his or her chair, desk, keyboard tray, and monitor faces fatigue and potentially serious injury, particularly in the form of carpal tunnel syndrome and other repetitive stress injuries. This illustration shows an example of a computer workstation that is designed to maximize the user's comfort and minimize the likelihood of injury.

The Universal Design Alliance, founded in 2003 and based in Suwanee, Georgia, outlines seven principles for developing and integrating universal design:

1. Equitable use: The design is useful and marketable to people with diverse abilities.
2. Flexible use: The design accommodates a wide range of individual preferences and abilities.
3. Simple and intuitive use: Use of the design is easy to understand, regardless of the user's experience, knowledge, language skills, or current concentration level.

4. Perceptible information: The design communicates necessary information effectively to the user, regardless of ambient conditions or the user's sensory abilities.
5. Tolerance for error: The design minimizes hazards and the adverse consequences of accidental or unintended actions.
6. Low physical effort requirement: The design can be used efficiently and comfortably and with a minimum of fatigue.
7. Size and space for approach and use: Appropriate size and space are provided for approach, reach, manipulation, and use regardless of user's body size, posture, or mobility.

In a similar vein, universal design for learning calls for multiple ways for learners to acquire knowledge; multiple alternatives for learners to demonstrate what they know; and multiple means of engagement, to tap into learners' interests, offer appropriate challenges, and increase motivation. While assistive technologies play a major role in the education of learners with disabilities, advocates of accessible technologies point out that these tools alone are insufficient. Universal design for learning does not eliminate the need for personal assistive devices, but universally accessible technology yields great rewards to the typical user as well. Good accessible design is universal design.

Notable examples of this principle include Apple's iPad and iPhone. These devices, with their innovative touch screens and intuitive interfaces, were not designed with adaptive technology in mind. Nevertheless, people with speech or other communication impairments, in particular the teachers and families of children with autism, are finding them to be remarkable communication tools. Autism is a disability that affects the way a person communicates and relates to other people and the world around them. Those affected typically display impairments in social interaction, communication, and behavior. Quite a few iPad and iPhone applications turn the devices into tools to help people on the autism spectrum interact more freely with the world around them. Some apps allow parents and educators to set up customized schedules, using personal voice recordings and images directly from their cameras. Others enable people with communication difficulties to express their needs and desires through a variety of images, pictures, symbols, and audio files.

(continues on page 136)

001101010010100111010110101010101100101000001

Victor Tsaran, Yahoo! Accessibility Engineer

Victor Tsaran was born in Vilnohirsk, Ukraine, and abandoned by his parents at the age of two. At five, he became completely blind as a result of a cataract operation. Until age 13, Victor lived in a Russian-speaking boarding school for the blind, a single building that contained the dormitory and classrooms. Orphan students left the school for special camps during the summer and stayed in the school during winter breaks with some of the dedicated teachers who opted to spend their holidays there.

Shortly after his eye surgery, Victor began playing the bayan, an accordion-style instrument with buttons instead of keys. He had also learned to play the sopilka, a Ukrainian folk wind instrument similar to a recorder, as well as some piano. At 12, he was shown a few guitar chords, which prompted his interest in learning to play the instrument. Although he studied Braille music when he was learning to play the bayan, Victor relied more on his ear when learning to play guitar, forgoing the Braille notation. He practiced relentlessly and taught himself guitar theory. At age 13, Victor was adopted by a couple from western Ukraine and moved to Lviv. Once there, he joined a succession of bands, playing at concerts and local festivals. In 1991, Victor won second prize in Acoustic Music at Chervona Ruta, a major Ukrainian music festival. He enrolled in Lviv University to study philosophy. During his second year, in 1994, Victor won a scholarship to attend the Overbrook School for the Blind in Philadelphia, Pennsylvania.

Victor's first trip to the United States to attend Overbrook changed his life by introducing him to his first computer. He had never touched a keyboard before, but after encountering computers that were able to communicate with him via speech synthesizers, he decided to study computer science instead of philosophy. Upon his return to Ukraine in 1996, Victor coestablished the first computer center for the blind in Lviv. He wanted to return to the United States after his scholarship year to earn a formal computer science degree. He won a scholarship from the Soros Foundation, which enabled him to attend Temple University in Philadelphia, where he enrolled in 1997.

Upon graduating in 2000 with a bachelor's degree in computer science, Victor traveled extensively for ON-NET (Overbrook Nippon Network on Educational Technology) in Southeast Asia, teaching computer skills to visually impaired users

001101010010100111010110101010101100101000001

of different ages. Victor has also held the position of accessibility manager at Bartimaeus Group in McLean, Virginia, where he was responsible for a variety of projects ranging from Section 508 compliance product testing to adapting proprietary software for disabled access.

Victor is currently the senior accessibility program manager at Yahoo! He oversees all accessibility activities, such as coding practices, policies, and training and awareness, throughout the company. Victor and his team focus on development of best practices for creation of Web sites that work well with screen readers.

Victor Tsaran, an accessibility engineer at Yahoo!, shown here working at his desk *(Used with the permission of Victor Tsaran)*

Screen reader software represents what is being displayed on the computer screen through image icons, Braille, or text-to-speech output, enabling a blind or vision-impaired user to interact with the machine. However, many Web sites are not easily accessible and do not work well with screen readers because they lack compatibility or contain heavy graphics, which slow the screen reader software. This happens partly because designers lack experience with accessibility issues and partly because accessibility features are often tacked on after a site is finished.

Yahoo! launched an accessibility lab in its Sunnyvale headquarters, as well as a second lab in Bangalore, India, where developers can experience the computer from the perspective of a disabled user. Victor's team worked on integrating accessibility features into the design process, as well as making Web advertisements accessible. In 2007, under the guidance of Victor and his research and development team in Bangalore, Yahoo! launched Yahoo! Mail Classic, which

(continues)

(continued)

is fully accessible to any user with any disability. Yahoo! Classic works with any standard screen reader software as well as screen magnifiers, allowing the visually impaired to check their e-mail and use the Internet. Other Yahoo! products, including Yahoo! IM, Yahoo! Finance, and Yahoo! Search, have also been enhanced to become fully accessible.

Victor's own experience as a blind computer user gives him a unique perspective into the design process. He frequently speaks about the importance of integrating accessibility into the fundamentals of design rather than bringing it in later in the process, as a crucial step in keeping accessibility current with new developments in Web design and other technological advances.

During his time in Philadelphia, Victor was introduced to bossa nova, which became an important influence in his musical development. Today, despite being heavily involved with accessibility research at Yahoo!, Victor composes and performs his own music, which he characterizes as soft jazz. He has recorded several albums in Ukrainian and performed concerts throughout Ukraine, Poland, and the United States. Victor is married to Karolina, a partially sighted fellow Overbrook student from Poland. They met while studying in Pennsylvania. Both Victor and Karolina remain involved with various accessibility organizations and publications.

(continued from page 133)

Although there are other computers designed for children with autism, a growing number of experts say the iPad is better. Proponents describe it as cheaper, faster, more versatile, more user-friendly, more portable, more engaging, and infinitely cooler. Technology critic John Gruber writes: "The iPad wasn't designed with autistic children in mind, but, anecdotally, the results are seemingly miraculous. My guess is that it has something to do with the lack of indirection—fingers touching screen elements directly, rather than pushing hardware buttons or manipulating an on-screen pointer using a mouse or trackpad."

CONCLUSIONS

The earliest computers did little to accommodate the needs of people with disabilities. The first personal computers provided only one input option—the keyboard—and two output options—the monitor and printer. Even features that today are taken for granted and not considered to be accessibility options, such as the ability to display text in multiple sizes or to have such text read aloud, were not available.

Recent years have seen significant growth in the number and variety of accessibility technologies that are available and affordable to the ordinary home computer user. Even technologically complex features, such as high-quality speech recognition software, now often come bundled with new computers or are built into computer operating systems so that such features are available for use in connection with all software on the computer at all times. Although some of these advances were made only reluctantly by computer hardware and software vendors in response to legal requirements, now that they are in place both technology companies and their users are coming to realize that options that begin as aids to those with disabilities can also make computers easier, safer, and more enjoyable for everyone.

7

FREEDOM OF SPEECH: IS THERE ANYTHING YOU CANNOT SAY?

Although freedom of speech is one of the most cherished values in any open society, it is also one of the most widely misunderstood and hotly debated, because the concepts of freedom and speech are so difficult to define. Even the staunchest defenders of freedom of speech recognize that people should not be free to threaten others with physical harm, and under criminal law such threats can constitute an assault even if they are not accompanied by any physical violence. Similarly, even the most strongly protected kinds of speech, such as criticism of the actions of government officials, are not protected by the legal right to freedom of speech under certain circumstances. For example, the law does not permit soldiers to publicly criticize the decisions of their superior officers during time of war. This chapter examines how developments in computer technology that make it possible to speak in new ways are raising difficult questions about how to apply the concept of freedom of speech to the Internet and how to preserve this freedom.

THE FIRST AMENDMENT

The U.S. Constitution did not contain an explicit protection for freedom of speech when it was first ratified in 1787. It was only in 1791, when the first 10 amendments to the Constitution—known as the Bill of Rights—were adopted, that freedom of speech obtained unambiguous legal protection in the United States. In particular, the first of these 10 amendments, the First Amendment, states in full that "Congress shall make no law respecting an establishment of religion, or prohibiting the free exercise thereof; or abridging the freedom of speech, or of the press; or the right of the people peaceably to assemble, and to petition

Patrick Henry, an orator, politician, and one of the Founding Fathers of the United States, is shown here arguing before the Virginia House of Burgesses on May 30, 1765. Henry is remembered as an ardent defender of freedom, particularly as a result of a famous speech in which he proclaimed, "Give me Liberty, or give me Death!"   *(Library of Congress)*

the Government for a redress of grievances." As can be seen from this text, the First Amendment protects several freedoms, including freedom of religion and freedom of the press. The portion of this text that states that "Congress shall make no law . . . abridging the freedom of speech" is known as the free speech clause because it protects freedom of speech.

In the beginning, the First Amendment did not protect freedom of speech as broadly as it does today. Instead, it only prohibited the Congress from passing federal laws that limited freedom of speech. It did not, for example, prohibit the president from issuing orders to censor the press, and it did not impose any limits on the ability of states to restrict freedom of speech. Furthermore, initially the First Amendment was interpreted to only prohibit Congress from using *prior restraints* to restrict speech. An example of a prior restraint is a law that prevents a newspaper from publishing in advance. Congress was allowed, however, to impose penalties, known as *subsequent punishments,* on speech after it occurred. In summary, when the First Amendment was adopted, it did little more than protect speakers against prior restraints by the Congress. Those who criticized the government in certain ways could still be convicted of the crime of sedition even after passage of the First Amendment.

Over time, the U.S. Supreme Court gradually expanded its interpretation of the First Amendment to provide increasingly broad protection for freedom of speech, such as by:

- applying the protections of the First Amendment to actions taken by the judicial and executive branches of the federal government, and to actions of state governments;
- prohibiting subsequent punishment of protected speech in addition to prior restraints;
- expanding the concept of "speech" to include not only spoken and printed words, but also artwork, music, film, and other forms of creative expression;
- prohibiting the government from censoring expression of viewpoints that it disagrees with but allowing voicing of opinions that it agrees with; and
- allowing entire statutes to be struck down as unconstitutional if they prohibited more protected speech than necessary.

Even after such expansion of the scope of the First Amendment, its protections against censorship extend only to restrictions imposed by government bodies and their officials. A private company, for example, can punish or fire its employees for criticizing the company without violating the First Amendment, even if the same speech would have been protected by the First Amendment if it had been uttered by a government employee about a government agency. This *state action* requirement is not well known outside of the legal profession and often leads to confusion about whether speech in a particular case is protected by the First Amendment.

The precise contours of the First Amendment have been defined by the Supreme Court in a large number of individual cases. As a result, there is no single, clear definition of what is protected by the First Amendment. Determining whether speech in a particular situation is protected requires reading and understanding all of the relevant Supreme Court cases and then applying them to the current circumstances. This makes it difficult even for legal experts to determine whether speech in borderline cases is protected. Although speech that is merely offensive (such as movies which depict violence, sex, or rude language) and speech that merely expresses an opinion critical of the government are always protected by the First Amendment, speech that calls for violent action to be taken and speech that reveals government secrets may or may not be protected by the First Amendment, depending on the circumstances. Therefore, those who plan to engage in such speech would do well to seek advice in advance from a lawyer before risking a fine or even prison for speaking in a way that violates a criminal law and that is not shielded by the First Amendment.

Despite the limitations of the First Amendment, its breadth and strength are notable in a world in which many governments continue to provide little if any legal protection to the speech of ordinary people. The fact that a private individual can publish an article denouncing the actions of the U.S. government, even during wartime, without facing any threat of civil or criminal penalties, is a testament to the high value placed on freedom of speech by the First Amendment.

FREE SPEECH IN RADIO AND TELEVISION

One might think at first that the development of a new communications medium, such as radio or television, would not require any changes to the interpretation of the First Amendment. If criticism of the government is protected and threats of violence are not protected, then it might seem that the same should automatically be true when the same speech is transmitted in a radio or television broadcast, rather than published in a newspaper. The U.S. Supreme Court, however, disagreed and, in a series of cases, has established different rules for speech on radio and television than in person and in print.

The Supreme Court's primary justification for treating broadcast speech differently than other speech for First Amendment purposes is that the electromagnetic spectrum available to transmit such broadcasts is inherently limited. No two broadcasts can be transmitted within the same region of the spectrum at the same time and in the same geographic area without interfering with each other. As a result, there is a limit to the number of broadcasts that can occur simultaneously in the same geographic region. Broadcast bandwidth, in other words, is scarce, distinguishing it from print media. There is no effective technological limit to the number of newspapers that can be printed and distributed in a particular city or state. The Supreme Court has concluded that, as a result of such scarcity, the federal government has an interest in ensuring that programs broadcast over the airwaves satisfy some minimal standards of promoting the public interest. This interest, according to the Supreme Court, justifies the federal government in imposing restrictions on radio and television broadcasts that would not be permissible to apply to newspapers, books, and other forms of nonbroadcast speech. As the Supreme Court stated in the case of *Red Lion v. FCC:* "Differences in the characteristics of new media justify differences in the First Amendment standards applied to them."

This *scarcity doctrine* has had several practical implications for radio and television broadcasters. One was the promulgation of the *fairness doctrine* by the Federal Communications Commission (FCC) beginning in 1947. The fairness doctrine required radio and television broadcasters to air presentations of

(opposite page) Transmissions by radio, television, and cellular telephone transmitters must each occupy their own range of signal bandwidth if they are not to interfere with each other before reaching a receiver. To avoid such overlaps, the U.S. government allocates different ranges of bandwidth frequencies to different kinds of communication and to particular parties (such as television and radio stations) within those ranges. This chart shows how just a small portion of the frequency spectrum is allocated among television, amateur radio, radio astronomy, land mobile radio, and mobile (e.g., cellular telephone) broadcasts. Regions of the spectrum denoted as fixed are allocated to particular parties at all times, whether or not those parties are making active use of their allocated spectrum at any particular time. Nonfixed regions of the spectrum may be made available to other parties when not otherwise in use.

controversial issues of importance to the public in such a way that was honest, equitable, and balanced. The Supreme Court acknowledged that the FCC had the power to enforce the fairness doctrine but did not hold that the FCC was required to do so. In 1987, Ronald Reagan abolished the fairness doctrine by

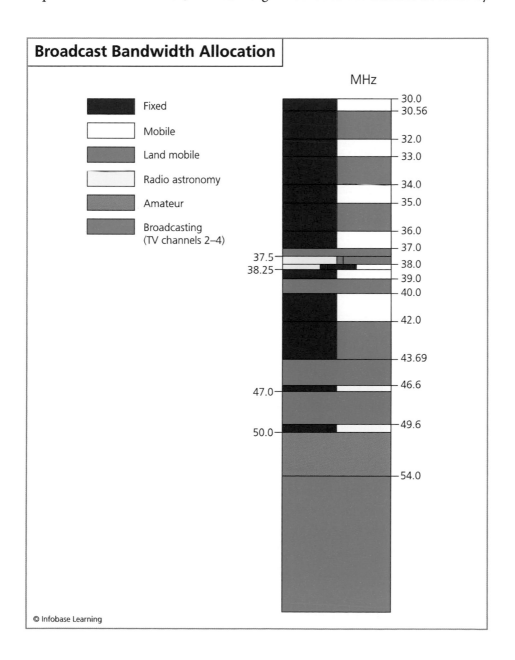

Broadcast Bandwidth Allocation

MHz

Fixed

Mobile

Land mobile

Radio astronomy

Amateur

Broadcasting
(TV channels 2–4)

30.0
30.56
32.0
33.0
34.0
35.0
36.0
37.0
37.5
38.0
38.25
39.0
40.0
42.0
43.69
46.6
47.0
49.6
50.0
54.0

George Carlin, Seven Dirty Words

Comedian George Carlin (1937–2008) is remembered for his irreverence, social and political satire, and his love of words. One of his most famous monologues uses the word "stuff" in nearly every sentence as a biting critique of consumer culture: "That's all your house is: a place to keep your stuff. If you didn't have so much stuff, you wouldn't need a house. You could just walk around all the time. A house is just a pile of stuff with a cover on it."

Carlin's "stuff" speech was incisive but not controversial. The same cannot be said of his more famous monologue about words, "Seven Words You Can Never Say on Television," which came to be known simply as the seven dirty words. In it, Carlin both recited the words—repeatedly—and analyzed them, their history, and their wide variety of common uses in great detail to draw attention to what he saw as the absurdity of banning them from television. He poked particular fun at the prohibition against any use of the words regardless of their context.

Carlin performed the routine in comedy clubs without incident. It was not until a recording of Carlin performing was broadcast by Pacifica radio station that the FCC upheld a complaint lodged by a man who heard the broadcast on his

executive order in favor of a policy that gave individual broadcasters the freedom to decide which views to air and how to do so.

The scarcity doctrine also resulted in several court decisions that gave the FCC authority to regulate *indecent speech* on radio and television, for the purpose of protecting children. Although the concept of indecency is notoriously difficult to define, the FCC has defined it as "language or material that, in context, depicts or describes, in terms patently offensive as measured by contemporary community standards for the broadcast medium, sexual or excretory organs or activities." Although indecent speech is not unprotected by the First Amendment, the FCC has authority to prohibit indecent speech from being broadcast during hours when children are likely to be listening or watching. The 1978 Supreme Court case that gave the FCC this authority, *Federal Communications Commission v. Pacifica Foundation,* was decided before the advent of the Web and even before VCRs became widespread. Many now consider the Supreme

`100111010010101010011001011101101010010101001`

radio while driving with his son. Pacifica appealed the case to the U.S. Supreme Court, which affirmed the FCC's decision in 1972 in *FCC v. Pacifica Foundation*. Ironically, Carlin's roast of overly zealous federal regulators had been turned against him, sealing into law the very restrictions that he had railed against. The *Pacifica* case and other cases established and refined the legal distinction between *obscene speech,* which is not protected by the First Amendment, and indecent speech, which is protected by the First Amendment but not considered suitable for minors and which therefore may be regulated although not entirely banned. For example, the Supreme Court has allowed television and radio broadcasters to air indecent speech (but not obscene speech) between 10 P.M. and 6 A.M., based on the premise that most children would not be awake during those hours.

In the years since the first broadcast of Carlin's performance, some of the seven dirty words have been used on U.S. broadcast television. Radio and television producers can never be entirely sure whether such uses will cause them to be fined by the FCC because the FCC has never published rules that clearly list specific prohibited words. Whether or not the seven dirty words may now be lawfully uttered on radio or television, out of an excess of caution they will not be reprinted here.

`100111010010101010011001011101101010010101001`

Court's decision in this case to be outdated in light of digital video recorders and the Internet, which largely make the time at which a program is transmitted independent of the time at which it is viewed by either children or adults.

FREE SPEECH ON THE INTERNET

As described earlier in this chapter, the FCC has defined indecent speech as "language or material that, in context, depicts or describes, in terms patently offensive as measured by contemporary community standards for the broadcast medium, sexual or excretory organs or activities." For example, speech that describes or depicts sex acts is typically considered indecent. It is lawful for the FCC to regulate the radio and television broadcast of such speech to reduce the likelihood that it will be heard or seen by children, typically by prohibiting indecent broadcasts between the hours of 6 A.M. and 10 P.M. At the same time, such speech is protected by the First Amendment. Therefore, the FCC cannot prohibit the broadcast of such speech entirely, because doing so would prohibit adults in the audience from receiving speech to which they are constitutionally entitled.

This delicate balancing act, in which indecent speech is broadcast only during certain hours of the day, depends on a set of assumptions about the technological features of radio and television broadcasts, namely that they are transmitted by a broadcaster at a particular time selected by the broadcaster and received essentially immediately by the entire audience simultaneously, and that they cannot be replayed at a later time of the audience's choosing. Although these assumptions were relatively valid through the 1970s, at least for television, they have become increasingly invalid in light of advances in technology for transmitting, receiving, recording, replaying, and redistributing radio, television, and other kinds of programs, both over the broadcast airwaves and the Internet.

The accompanying sidebar on attorney Ann Beeson describes some of the ways in which attempts by the U.S. Congress to regulate speech on the Internet have been struck down by the courts as inconsistent with the First Amendment. In general, the courts have concluded that although scarcity of transmission frequencies justifies regulating speech on television and radio, such scarcity does not exist on the Internet, which allows a nearly unlimited number of people to speak simultaneously.

When one person creates a new Web site, this does not prevent anyone else from posting another Web site that is viewable by the same audience in the same place at the same time. Speech on the Internet, therefore, is more free of regulation than speech on radio and television.

Legal considerations aside, the Internet is technologically more difficult to regulate than print, radio, and television. In fact, early Internet visionaries imagined that the technology underlying the Internet would make it completely immune to any kind of censorship. Electronic Frontier Foundation (EFF) founder and Internet activist John Gilmore proclaimed in 1993 that the "Net interprets censorship as damage and routes around it," alluding to the fact that attempts to block e-mail and other forms of Internet communication would not in fact prevent such communications from reaching their destination, but only cause them to take alternate paths along the way. Similarly, another EFF founder and former Grateful Dead lyricist John Perry Barlow wrote, in his 1996 manifesto, "A Declaration of the Independence of Cyberspace," that governments

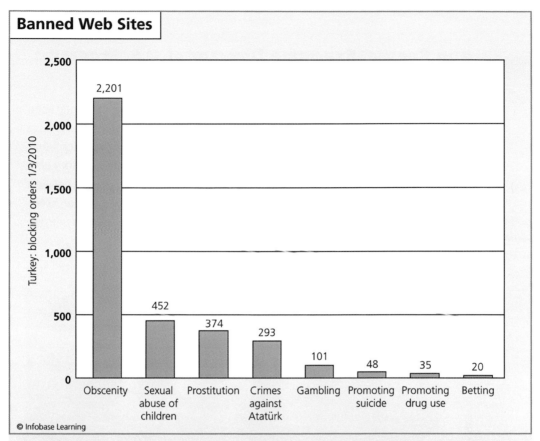

Banned Web Sites

Turkey: blocking orders 1/3/2010

Obscenity	2,201
Sexual abuse of children	452
Prostitution	374
Crimes against Atatürk	293
Gambling	101
Promoting suicide	48
Promoting drug use	35
Betting	20

© Infobase Learning

Government policies for determining which Web sites are banned vary significantly from country to country. This chart shows, as an example, the number and types of Web sites blocked by the Turkish government, by both court decisions and administrative decisions as of January 3, 2010.

"are not welcome among us" and "have no sovereignty where we gather." Barlow went so far as to assert that governments "have no moral right to rule us" in cyberspace and that they do not "possess any methods of enforcement we have true reason to fear."

These early pronouncements that governments would be powerless to censor speech on the Internet or otherwise control cyberspace seem exaggerated and naïve in retrospect, in light of the continued successes of repressive governments at banning Web sites. The claims of John Gilmore and John Perry

(continues on page 150)

001101010010100111010110101010101011001010000 1

Ann Beeson, Executive Director of U.S. Programs at the Open Society Institute

Ann Beeson is a human rights advocate and distinguished litigator, currently serving as the executive director of U.S. Programs at the Open Society Institute. Beeson grew up in Dallas, where her mother was a high school teacher and her father worked as a Sears Roebuck credit manager. She is a 1993 graduate of Emory University Law School, where she was editor in chief of the *Emory Law Journal,* and also holds a master's degree in cultural anthropology from the University of Texas. Beeson was named among *National Law Journal*'s 50 most influential women lawyers in 2007 and was also featured in *American Lawyer*'s 50 rising legal stars under 45. She is also an amateur pilot, jazz aficionado, and singer.

Ann Beeson, civil liberties lawyer, shown here talking to the press in Detroit about a legal challenge by the American Civil Liberties Union (ACLU) to the federal government's wiretapping policy *(AP Images)*

001101010010100111010110101010101011001010000 1

10011101001010101001100101110110101001010101

Although both her parents were conservative Republicans, Beeson could not be more devoted to liberal causes. She first became interested in free speech and the Internet as a law student. After graduating from law school, she spent a year as a clerk to U.S. district court judge Harold Barefoot Sanders, Jr., in Texas and accepted a one-year fellowship to work at Human Rights Watch. However, before she had a chance to finish her fellowship, Beeson became involved with the American Civil Liberties Union (ACLU), which had then begun following cyberspace issues. Beeson was curious about what effects the Internet would have on free speech and accepted a one-year fellowship on cyberspace legal issues with the ACLU in February 1995. The same year, Congress began extensive debates on the merits of a law that would restrict Internet speech.

Beeson started her ACLU career as a lobbyist trying to prevent the passage of the Communications Decency Act (CDA), which was eventually passed by Congress in 1996. When it became obvious that the CDA was going to be passed, she started working with the legal department on putting together a case to challenge it. *Reno v. ACLU* became Beeson's first case. The ACLU, together with 19 other plaintiffs, challenged the CDA's online censorship provisions that sought to criminalize "indecent" and "patently offensive" communications directed at minors. These provisions were invalidated by a three-judge panel in a Pennsylvania district court. The government appealed that decision to the Supreme Court, which in 1997 found that major portions of the CDA were unconstitutional because they violated the First Amendment right to free speech, and upheld the lower court's ruling. *Reno v. ACLU* was the first case that sought to place limits on online communications and that held that such limits were unconstitutional.

In 2001, Beeson was the lead attorney and argued in front of the Supreme Court in the case of *Ashcroft v. ACLU,* Congress's second attempt at regulating Internet speech with the *Child Online Protection Act (COPA),* which sought to prevent minors from being able to access pornography online. The ACLU sued to prevent enforcement of the act and secured a favorable verdict in the federal district court, successfully arguing that COPA violated the free speech clause of the First Amendment and that parents—not the government—should be responsible for restricting children's access to pornography and other inappropriate information online. On appeal, the Third Circuit Court of Appeals affirmed the district

(continues)

10011101001010101001100101110110101001010101

(continued)

court's ruling, and the government appealed to the Supreme Court, which in 2004 ruled in favor of the ACLU.

Beeson also filed challenges to the USA PATRIOT Act on behalf of journalists, scholars, and nonprofit organizations, arguing that the National Security Agency's warrantless surveillance of e-mail and phone conversations within the United States violated the First and Fourth Amendments to the Constitution. The federal district court ruled in favor of the ACLU, but the Sixth Circuit Court of Appeals dismissed the case, and the Supreme Court refused to review the lower court's decision.

In June 2007, Beeson left the ACLU and joined the Open Society Institute (OSI) as the director of U.S. programs. OSI is a part of the network of foundations created and funded by American financier George Soros. Founded in 1993, OSI seeks to strengthen democracy and promote equality and human rights. It is most famous in the United States for funding and supporting after-school inner-city programs and urban debate leagues. Beginning in late 2007, OSI funded advocacy efforts to help those most affected by the financial and subprime mortgage crisis. Under Beeson's watch, OSI funded the Neighborhood Stabilization Initiative in New York, which assists homeowners in renegotiating their loans and helps prevent evictions and foreclosures. Together with Atlantic Philanthropies, OSI is participating in and lending resources to the initiative to support nonprofit grantee organizations that lost funding when the JEHT foundation, many of whose donors' funds were mismanaged by Bernard Madoff, was forced to close.

(continued from page 147)

Barlow do, however, point out a significant feature of the Internet, even if not as starkly as they originally imagined: Anyone with a computer and an Internet connection can make anything that he or she wants to say available to the world instantly, easily, and at almost no cost, at the click of a mouse.

The mere legal right to speak on the Internet and the ability to make one's speech available on the Internet, however, does not guarantee that one's speech will be heard by anyone, much less by the whole world. The sheer volume of information available on the Internet can make it difficult for any single voice to rise above the noise. Taking blogs as an example, there were already more than 10 million blogs in 2004 and more than 70 million blogs in 2007. It was estimated that 175,000 new blogs were being created every day in 2008. Most services that previously tracked these numbers no longer bother to do so because the numbers are so large and are increasing so rapidly. Savvy Internet marketers use software to automatically generate blogs that copy content from other blogs to create what appears to be a collection of original blog postings, but in reality consist entirely of copied content designed to draw readers to click on paid advertisements. In such an environment, a hobbyist blogger who posts her own short stories, news articles, or journal entries may fail to reach interested readers because it is impossible for readers to sift through the haystack of heavily funded commercial blogs and artificially generated blog links to find anything.

Although everyone may have a First Amendment right to speak on the Internet and the technological ability to publish their speech to the Web, there is no guarantee that one's speech, once released into cyberspace, will be heard. This may be one reason why many are turning away from the generic Web to social networking sites as a way to share their thoughts, because such sites combine the freedom and power of the Web with the ability to direct one's ideas and feelings directly to one's existing community and to engage in conversations with members of those communities without first having to weed through the clutter of the wide-open Web.

CONCLUSIONS

Legal protection for freedom of speech, at least in the United States, has come full circle as a result of the Internet. Before the advent of electronic communication in the form of the telegraph, telephone, radio, and television, the technological means used to deliver speech did not have a significant impact on the legal protection afforded to that speech. The 20th century then saw a fracturing of legal protection for speech, with a different set of legal rules being applied to each form of communication technology. Now that the Internet has eliminated the technological limitations associated with older forms of communication, the legal barriers have broken down significantly in response.

In addition to this opening in the law, computer and Internet technology have provided significant boosts to the power of both professional and amateur authors, artists, musicians, and filmmakers to create and distribute their works. Although this has created a flood of content, which some might liken to a plague due to the high volume of low-quality material it contains, efforts are underway to make it easier to filter, evaluate, sort, and present Internet content in ways that benefits creators and audiences equally. The news aggregator Google News is one such example. Google News automatically sorts thousands of news articles into groups of articles about the same topic, and presents such groups to Web users in a well-organized, visually pleasing format. Although the software that powers Google News might favor some topics or news providers over others, readers always have the option of formulating their own query for news articles instead of relying on the judgment of Google's software. Similar aggregators exist for nearly every kind of content, from music to film to magazine articles. Some of them harness the expertise of human editors in addition to, or instead of, the conclusions drawn by software algorithms. This return to the philosophy that forms the foundation of traditional journals, newspapers, and magazines, but with a new technological twist, is yet one more way in which freedom of speech may be coming full circle on the Internet.

8

FROM ONE-TO-ONE TO MANY-TO-MANY: THE WIDE REACH OF COMPUTER COMMUNICATION

Communication does not only take place between one speaker and one listener. Sometimes, one speaker speaks and many people listen, as in the case of a politician on the stump campaigning for office. As another example, sometimes many authors contribute to a work that is read by a single reader, as in the case of a grant proposal submitted by a committee to a wealthy donor. In yet other situations, many speakers have many listeners, as in the case of a team of scientists who present their findings to an audience of their peers at a conference. This chapter explores just a few of the ways in which computers and the Internet are updating and expanding the variety of ways in which people can communicate and collaborate with each other to encompass almost every permutation imaginable.

ONE-TO-ONE

Human lives are filled with, perhaps even defined by, communication between individuals. When someone calls a friend, texts a classmate, or sends an e-mail, another link is forged in a chain of one-to-one communication that has existed as long as there has been someone to talk and someone to listen. This contact between people can be as high-tech as an instant message sent via a wireless Internet connection or as low-tech as a handwritten letter.

Regardless of the technology used, one-to-one communication tends to have a particularly intimate feel, even when conducted over long distances and over time. When the

Pony Express was operating in the early 1860s, it took about 10 days for riders to carry a letter 1,966 miles from the base in St. Joseph, Missouri, to the terminus in Sacramento, California. To reach the East Coast from St. Joseph took another week or so, for a total delivery time of 14 to 18 days. That was a blazing speed at a time when mail delivery via steamship or stagecoach could take more than a month. In contrast, instant messaging, e-mail, and video conferencing provide a practically instantaneous connection.

People always have and probably always will seek out one-to-one communication in the context of close personal relationships or to seek advice, comfort, or consolation. One-to-one communication allows a message to be tailored specifically to the personality, language, and situation of one's audience, lending clarity and preventing misunderstanding. Meaning-filled behaviors occur in both the expressive and receptive roles, adding context and amplifying the message. When speaking or writing to another person, one's word choices, manner, energy, and attitude convey far more than words alone. Likewise, the person on the other end must do more than passively receive a message—paying attention, giving feedback, and interpreting meaning all are active undertakings.

The telephone is one of the oldest forms of one-to-one telecommunications technology and remains one of the most widely used forms of electronic communication, precisely because it provides an experience that closely resembles face-to-face contact. E-mail, text messaging, and online chat often seem shallow and distant in comparison to a telephone call when one seeks to share an accomplishment or vent about a frustrating experience. The technology that makes telephone calls possible has changed significantly since the days of Alexander Graham Bell and even since the introduction of the cellular telephone. For many decades, telephone technology was implemented using the *public switched telephone network (PSTN)* topology. According to this scheme, first devised by AT&T, the various switches within the telephone network were organized into five classes of switches, each of which would generally reside in an office or other centralized location.

Beginning with the switches closest to the customer placing the telephone call, the class 5 office, also referred to as the "local exchange" or "end office," delivered a dial tone to the customer. Typically, the first three digits in a seven-digit telephone number were associated with a single local exchange. The purpose of the class 4 office, also referred to as the "toll center," "toll point," or "intermediate point," was to route calls between two end offices that have no

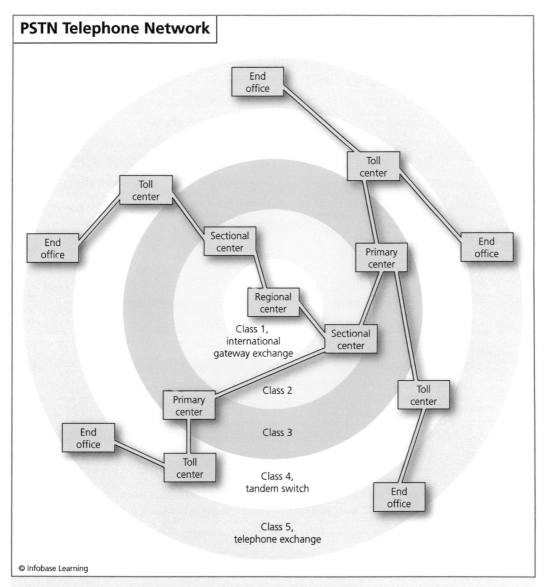

PSTN Telephone Network

End office

Toll center

Toll center

End office

Sectional center

Primary center

End office

Regional center

Class 1, international gateway exchange

Sectional center

Class 2

Primary center

Toll center

End office

Class 3

End office

Toll center

Class 4, tandem switch

End office

Class 5, telephone exchange

© Infobase Learning

The public switched telephone network (PSTN), also referred to as the plain old telephone service (POTS), is the network of the world's public circuit-switched telephone networks, which provides telephone service to most of the people with telephone service in the world.

direct connection with each other. The development of the class 4 office, therefore, was an important step in enabling any two telephones within a city or town to make calls to each other.

The class 3 office, also known as the "primary center," enabled calls to be made beyond the geographical boundaries defined by the connections between class 4 offices. Class 3 offices made it possible for telephones to be connected within larger geographic regions. At the height of the use of the PSTN, between 150 and 230 class 3 offices existed in the United States and Canada. The class 2 office, also known as the sectional center, connected major toll centers to enable long-distance telephone calls, such as calls between states. Finally, the class 1 office, also known as the regional center, served both as a backup in the case of failure of class 1–4 offices and as a way to block calls in the event that too many calls were being made simultaneously within the network.

ONE-TO-MANY

Of course, communication sometimes happens on a larger scale than one-to-one, when it is desirable for a large group of people to hear the same message. One-to-many communication may alert people to danger, entertain them, or convey news that concerns the entire group. The mass media are a form of one-to-many communication, as are many Web sites, e-mail newsletters, and blogs. People have long used one-to-many communication for a variety of reasons:

- It is often the most efficient way to reach many people at once. Transmitting a message a single time is easier than sending the same message individually to many people.
- It can ensure a clear message. Think of the children's game of "telephone," when a phrase is transmitted in whispers from person to person, usually winding up as a hilariously altered version of the original. If people hear a message for themselves, rather than relying on a second- or thirdhand version, the chances are much lower that the meaning will be distorted.
- It can be the path of least resistance. In some situations, it takes effort not to communicate to many people. When at home with family, in a crowded room, or out on the street, sometimes just speaking to one person will, as a side effect, transmit the message to multiple people.
- It offers economies of scale. Mass media, such as newspapers, radio, and television, require large and expensive equipment. It makes eco-

nomic sense to purchase and run such equipment only if it is used to reach a wide audience.

"One-to-many" communication can be remarkably low-tech—think of long-ago people telling stories with paintings on a cave wall or a town crier alerting villagers to the latest news. In ancient China, soldiers stationed along the Great Wall would alert each other of an impending enemy attack by sending smoke signals from tower to tower. Even today, the College of Cardinals in Rome uses smoke signals to indicate the selection of a new pope.

One-to-many communication can move an audience to tears, make them laugh, or spur them to action. One classic example of great verbal communication is Dr. Martin Luther King, Jr.'s I Have a Dream speech, filled with powerful visual images that provoke strong emotions and delivered with passion by some-

Frederic Remington's painting, *The Smoke Signal,* depicts Native Americans' use of patterns of smoke to communicate over long distances.   *(Peter Newark American Pictures/Bridgeman Art Library)*

one who captured the dreams of an entire generation. Over time, the speech has transcended its original message to be a message of hope for all people.

There are also some disadvantages to this type of communication:

- The intimacy and personal understanding of a one-to-one relationship is lost.
- The message is not tailored to individual recipients. As a result, it may be geared to the lowest common denominator or misunderstood by some of the audience.
- Direct feedback from audience to communicator is unavailable. As a result, the communicator cannot learn from the audience, at least not immediately. (New technologies, however, may be changing this in some instances.)
- In traditional media, one-to-many has high up-front and ongoing costs. This can lead to the generation of content to appeal to the masses and produce maximum profit.

Online publishing is changing the traditional mass media model. It strips out many of the costs associated with print publishing or broadcasting. Online publications can be viable with far fewer subscribers, and the start-up process is cheap and quick. The cost of Internet delivery continues to fall as storage, hosting, and bandwidth decrease in price, and distribution in the offline world continues to rise as paper costs, overhead, and postage increase. Timeliness is another area where online publishing has the advantage. In a world of rapid change and instant gratification, the information sources that react most quickly to events will become the most popular.

MANY-TO-ONE

If interpersonal communication operates on a one-to-one basis and larger-scale communication functions as one-to-many, a third type of communication can be characterized as many-to-one. Traditional examples might include a bookstore in which publications from many authors or publishers are available to individual customers or a poll that gathers data from a broad study group. The process of democratic government, in which citizens make their opinions known by choosing candidates or voting on a referendum, is another form of many-to-one communication. New developments in online media have created a growing body of opportunities for many-to-one communication. The term *individuation* is used to describe online technologies that allow individual users to customize the contents of newspapers, magazines, television programs, or Web sites to match their unique interests. Think of pay-per-view cable TV channels, Web sites, or digital recording devices that let viewers watch their favorite shows not just when they are broadcast, but when it is convenient to the viewer.

Crowdsourcing, in journalism, relies on a large group of readers to help report a news story. It differs from traditional reporting in that the information collected is gathered not by a reporter, but through some automated agent, such as a Web site. The reader-contributed reports can be collected, analyzed, and published in real time. Journalists are developing standards to ensure the veracity of crowdsourced information, such as requiring registration, e-mail verification, zip codes, or name and address. Obviously false information can be flagged for easy deletion. The public has the opportunity to dispute or verify individual reports, through comments or by posting alternative information. Crowdsourcing asks readers to do nothing more than serve as eyewitnesses to their daily lives—they need not learn advanced reporting skills or journalism ethics. Nor does it allow a single contributor's work to stand on its own, without the context of many additional points of view. In crowdsourcing, individual responses are of secondary importance to the larger data set.

The use of crowdsourcing extends beyond journalism. Some innovative examples:

- The U.S. Geological Survey (USGS) has a "Did You Feel It" feature that creates detailed "shake maps" to illustrate the intensity of earthquakes by zip code, through thousands of volunteer reports submitted online by the public. <earthquake.usgs.gov/earthquakes/dyfi>
- GasBuddy.com, which allows residents of more than 100 communities to share real-time reports on gas prices in their area. <www.gasbuddy.com>
- Commercial enterprises like iStockPhoto or MusicRevolution allow communities of photographers and musicians to make their work

available to consumers. Each submission enriches and expands the available offerings, and the creators and services share royalties from the sale of licensed content. <www.istockphoto.com or www. musicrevolution.com>

Popular social communities such as Flickr, YouTube, Facebook, and Digg, as well as the vast array of music-sharing communities, combine elements of online community-based communications, such as individual relationships and message-based conversations, with collective many-to-one interactions, such as voting, recommendations, and rankings. Individual choices, opinions, or experiences are collected to reveal the interests of the mass population. As an example, many consumers have learned to take advantage of the comment or review features on restaurant listings, hotel booking sites, or retail sites such as Amazon. However, smart shoppers also know that they must be critical users of that information, and some reviews must be taken with a grain of salt. If an online community is viewed as one that facilitates production and consumption of information, both producers and consumers now enjoy better understanding of the other side. As more consumers share their opinions, producers can also observe their aggregate preferences. Instead of simply visiting a site or buying a product, consumers can now become part of the community and let their voices be heard.

Sometimes those voices can produce surprising consequences. Blogs and online news programs were buzzing in fall 2010, when comedian, writer, and musician Steve Martin made an appearance at the 92nd Street Y in Manhattan. Midway through the discussion, a Y employee brought interviewer Deborah Solomon, a former *New York Times* columnist, a note that directed her to steer the conversation away from Martin's latest novel and focus on his more popular career as an actor. The request was the result of numerous real-time complaints the Y received via e-mail from audience members. Following the event, the Y offered all audience members a refund. The *New York Times* reported that the Y sent this message to its guests: "We planned for a more comprehensive discussion and we, too, were disappointed with the evening. We will be mailing you a $50 certificate for each ticket you purchased to last night's event. The gift certificate can be used toward future 92Y events, pending availability."

WIKIPEDIA

New media is a broad term that emerged in the latter part of the 20th century to describe the combined power of traditional media with interactive communications technology, most particularly the Internet. An important premise of new media is the democratization of the publishing process. Wikipedia, the online encyclopedia, is a prime example of this phenomenon.

Created in January 2001, Wikipedia combines Internet-accessible digital text, images, and video with Web links, interactive user feedback, and an active community of writers and editors. It describes itself as "a multilingual, Web-based, free-content encyclopedia project based on an openly editable model." The name is a portmanteau of the words *wiki* (a technology for creating collaborative Web sites, from the Hawaiian word meaning "quick") and encyclopedia. Wikipedia's articles are written by largely anonymous Internet volunteers working collaboratively. Anyone with Internet access can write or revise an article.

The guiding principles of the project are called the five pillars:

- Wikipedia is an online encyclopedia.
- Wikipedia has a neutral point of view.
- Wikipedia is free content that anyone can edit and distribute.
- Wikipedians should interact in a respectful and civil manner.
- Wikipedia does not have firm rules.

The Wikipedia community is largely self-organizing; anyone may become involved in any role, subject to peer approval. Individuals may choose to review articles, monitor articles for vandalism, or enforce quality control. A variety of software-assisted systems and automated programs help editors and administrators watch for problematic contributions and participants. Wikipedia also has a style and content manual and a variety systems for continual article review and improvement.

Compare the process of developing Wikipedia with that of the *Encyclopaedia Britannica*. This traditional reference work is made up of the contributions of hundreds of writers and editors, chosen carefully for their expertise in specific fields. Their articles are carefully reviewed by other experts and editors before appearing in the encyclopedia's print or online versions. This is a highly

(continues on page 164)

Ubiquitous Computing

When the field of ubiquitous computing originated in the late 1980s, it sounded a bit like a science fiction fantasy: Proponents imagined technology blending seamlessly into almost every aspect of people's lives. Instead of turning on a desktop or laptop, people would turn to high-tech tools integrated into everyday objects, even the air itself. Mark Weiser, regarded as the founder of the field, described it this way: "Ubiquitous computing names the third wave in computing, just now beginning. First were mainframes, each shared by lots of people. Now we are in the personal computing era, person and machine staring uneasily at each other across the desktop. Next comes ubiquitous computing, or the age of calm technology, when technology recedes into the background of our lives."

In Weiser's vision, the boundaries between technology and the social world were blurred. Computers would sense users' presence and act accordingly. The scenarios ranged from the fantastic to the prosaic, such as coffeemakers starting up when the morning alarm went off, visible electronic trails following people as they pass through a neighborhood, or the swipe of a pen transmitting a newspaper article from home to office. People themselves could be tracked by badges or other devices, and e-mail could be automatically forwarded to them. Mobile computers would be designed to interact with users and with this digital environment. From a human point of view, the technology would blend into the background and augment abilities.

Ubiquitous computing—sometimes shortened to ubicomp—is unusual among fields of technological research. Computer science is usually defined by technological problems and solutions. Ubiquitous computing, by contrast, is driven not so much by the problems of the past but by the possibilities of the future. Some researchers say that future has already arrived.

A National Public Radio preview of the 2011 Consumer Electronics Show in Las Vegas, Nevada, featured products such as Internet-connected television sets and refrigerators that alert their owners when the milk runs low. The Ford Motor Company was showing off a Car of the Future prototype equipped with Internet radio, voice-activated e-mail messaging, and a store for purchasing in-car software. More and more people use smart phones, which allow them to walk around with computers in their pockets, wirelessly connected to the vast capabili-

Ubiquitous Computing

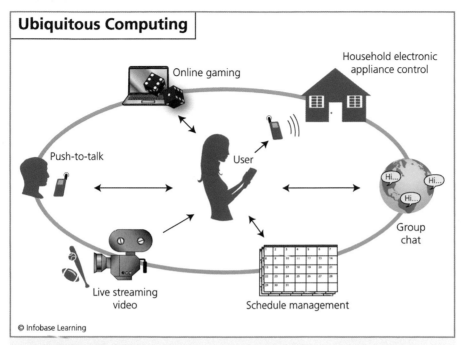

Online gaming

Household electronic appliance control

Push-to-talk

User

Group chat

Live streaming video

Schedule management

© Infobase Learning

Although at one time each person used one or perhaps two stationery computers located at a desk, now computer users have access to computers in many forms—such as desktop computers, laptop computers, smart phones, digital cameras, and global positioning system (GPS) receivers—at nearly all times. The logical conclusion of this increasingly widespread availability of computers is ubiquitous computing, according to which computers will be everywhere and always connected to each other over the Internet. One challenge of ubiquitous computing is ensuring that computers do not become more intrusive as they become more available.

ties of the Internet. If a person chooses, his friends on Facebook and FourSquare can follow along with what he is reading and where he decides to have dinner. The role of everyday technology in the early 21st century is already quite different than Weiser envisioned nearly three decades ago. Devices with wireless data communication and powerful computational capabilities are certainly ubiquitous in modern society. And increasingly, ubiquitous computing poses questions of social, personal, privacy, and environmental issues.

(continued from page 161)

mediated work—many eyes and minds examine and modify each article on its way to publication. Thus many people around the world regard *Britannica* as a respected, authoritative source.

Alternatively, Wikipedia is continually created and updated, with articles on historic events appearing within minutes, rather than months or years. It attracts nearly 78 million visitors a month. More than 91,000 active contributors are working on more than 17 million articles in more than 270 languages. It uses a less formal form of mediation that relies on collaboration and computer technology. The dynamic nature of Wikipedia has presented a challenge to established methods of academic research. Many educators regard it as an unreliable source but acknowledge that it can be a valuable tool for gathering information or as a starting point for research.

As with all reference works, not everything found in Wikipedia is accurate, comprehensive, or unbiased. General good-sense guidelines for conducting research apply:

- Beware of single sources or of multiple works that derive from a single source.
- If an article refers to external sources, read the references and verify that they support what the article says.
- In most academic institutions, references to Wikipedia, along with other encyclopedias, are unacceptable for a research paper.

In some notable incidents, users have intentionally placed misinformation on Wikipedia. A 2005 controversy known as the Seigenthaler incident began with the anonymous posting of a hoax article about John Seigenthaler, a well-known American journalist. The post falsely claimed that Seigenthaler had been a suspect in the assassinations of President John F. Kennedy and Attorney General Robert F. Kennedy. The 78-year-old Seigenthaler, who had been a friend and aide to Robert Kennedy and a pallbearer at his funeral, characterized the Wikipedia entry in a newspaper article as "Internet character assassination." The culprit was eventually revealed as Brian Chase of Nashville, Tennessee, who had created the hoax entry as a prank on a colleague. The entry was corrected, and Chase sent a written apology to Seigenthaler. After the incident, Wikipedia announced that unregistered users would no longer be allowed to create new articles.

Other incidents have been more lighthearted. Political satirist Stephen Colbert, star of cable television's "Colbert Report," once urged his audience to alter the Wikipedia entry on elephants by stating that the world's pachyderm population had tripled in the last six months. Scores of Internet users took him up on it, repeatedly vandalizing approximately 20 articles on elephants. The articles were eventually locked by administrators, and user "Stephencolbert" was blocked. Wikipedia's founder, Jimmy Wales, regarded the incident philosophically. "It's fine," he told a reporter. "We have a sense of humor, and if we wanted to, we could figure out if it was really him making the changes. But why bother? We banned the user because of his or her behavior, because they were messing around with some articles and encouraging other people to mess with several articles about elephants." Nor was Wales worried that Colbert's prank would undermine the site's credibility. "We try as hard as we can to make sure every piece of information on the site is backed up by verifiable sources, and if something is under dispute, we remove it until people can provide us with sources," he said. "Also, I've met Stephen, and I know how he is. He likes to have a joke."

ARE WE TOO CONNECTED? A DAY UNPLUGGED

The computer and telecommunications industries have long sought to make it possible for any two people, anywhere in the world, to communicate in any way at any time. Today's technology has come close to achieving this goal. Two people with Internet-connected computers can now send e-mail messages to each other, talk using Skype or other VoIP services, and chat over Facebook at any time. Even two people who only have cell phones can likely reach each other, regardless of the countries in which they are located, as long as they are willing to pay the required fee. Wireless broadband Internet service is spreading throughout the globe, thereby eliminating the need to use a cable to connect to an Internet access point.

As a result of this ability to be connected always, many are not only allowing themselves to be reached at all hours of the day and night but are actively initiating communications everywhere and anywhere. Couples dining at a restaurant may forgo face-to-face conversation by using their Blackberries to text with their friends across the country. Students in a classroom may use their laptops to shop online, unbeknown to their teachers. Lawyers in a courtroom may check for urgent messages back at the office while their adversaries present their arguments to judge and jury.

Efforts have been made to curb some of the negative consequences of such overuse of Internet-based communications, although with limited success. Restaurants post signs pleading with their customers to turn those cell phones off while dining. High schools and colleges ban Web browsing in the classroom. Some theaters, hospitals, and courthouses have even installed technology that blocks cell phone signals within certain rooms.

Yet such external efforts to impose limits on electronic communications only avoid the more pressing question: Should individuals impose limits on themselves. Several recent books indicate that there may be good reason to do so:

- *The Shallows: What the Internet Is Doing to Our Brains,* by Nicholas Carr, documents how excessive use of e-mail, text messaging, and Web browsing can cause physical changes in the brains of computer users that lead to loss of ability to concentrate on any task for an extended period of time.
- *Distracted: The Erosion of Attention and the Coming Dark Age,* by Maggie Jackson, explains how addiction to multitasking and the Internet is eroding the ability to engaged in deep, sustained, perceptive attention and standing in the way of the development of intimate human relationships.
- *The Dumbest Generation: How the Digital Age Stupefies Young Americans and Jeopardizes Our Future (Or, Don't Trust Anyone Under 30),* by Mark Bauerlein, documents how relying solely on the Internet as a source of information to the exclusion of long-form textual works such as scholarly books and journal articles is leading to a generation of young people who excel at absorbing large numbers of individual facts but who lack the ability to combine those facts into a synthetic whole.

Constant Internet communication has become so commonplace that it is now considered unusual, even abnormal, to consciously disconnect from the Internet for an extended period of time—where extended may be as little as an hour in some social circles. In fact, Susan Maushart obtained significant media

(continues on page 170)

James, "Jimbo" Wales, Cofounder of Wikipedia

Jimmy Wales was born in Huntsville, Alabama, in 1966. He attended a small private school and earned a bachelor's degree in finance from Auburn University and a master's degree from the University of Alabama. In 1994, Wales took a job with Chicago Options Associates, an options and trading firm in Chicago. After attaining the position of research director, Wales quit and started an Internet portal called Bomis. Although Bomis was not very successful, it provided Wales with enough money for his next project. In 1999, together with philosopher Larry Sanger as editor in chief, Wales launched Nupedia, an open-content online

(continues)

Jimmy "Jimbo" Wales, founder of online encyclopedia Wikipedia   *(© Rick Friedman/ Corbis)*

(continued)

encyclopedia. Nupedia struggled to attract attention and had just 12 articles after 18 months of online existence. Having been told of a relatively unknown piece of software called a "wiki," which means "quick" in Hawaiian, Sanger and Wales set up Wikipedia, which was meant to funnel content to Nupedia by allowing anyone to write, edit, and track changes to articles using the wiki software. Unexpectedly, the ease of using wiki software attracted a lot of attention to and turned Wikipedia into an overnight success. Wales and Sanger shut down Nupedia to concentrate on Wikipedia alone.

Wikipedia is a not-for-profit encyclopedia resource that contains articles of free content and may be reproduced without seeking and paying a permission fee. There are several versions of wiki software, which has been around since the mid-1990s; Wikipedia uses the MediaWiki software to run its pages. Wiki software supports hyperlinks, which allow its articles to be interlinked, as well as simple text that allows even a nontechnically advanced user to create an entry. Wikipedia is managed by the Wikimedia Foundation, a not-for-profit organization set up by Wales in 2003 to handle Wikipedia and its sister projects, such as Wiktionary, Wikianswers, Wikibooks, and others. Wikimedia is supported by donations and through fund-raising and operates Wikipedia through a nonprofit, leanly staffed San Francisco, California, office. Wales has also formed a for-profit company called Wikia, which hosts a collection of individual wikis on different subjects and is meant to promote software for creating wikis.

Wikipedia is run by a group of volunteers, but anyone can contribute an article or make edits to an existing article, with a few exceptions. Each article has a "Page History" link, which tracks all changes that have been made to the individual entry. Users who come across errors in entries are encouraged to correct them. This is intended to keep information on Wikipedia both current and accurate. Similarly, those uncertain or confused by the material are encouraged to leave a question on Wikipedia "talk" page to be answered by the next person who knows the answer and can correct the entry to be more straightforward and accurate. Wikipedia has created a community of Wikipedians who are registered with the site and are active through e-mail and constant monitoring of changes to Wikipedia's articles through the Recent Changes page. They are quick to correct erroneous or malicious edits to articles, which sometimes are made to pages covering current events or articles about particularly inflammatory topics. However, one does not need to create a Wikipedia registration to edit an article, although creating an article and editing some of the more controversial articles or current events articles are limited to registered users. Most active Wikipedians—those who have made at least 1,000 contributions—can become administrators. To become one, they must pass through a vetting process, during which any Wikipedia user can question them on their knowledge of copyright and libel law.

Wikipedia has had some struggles with the accuracy of its entries and is working on improving quality control or at least a way to note that a particular article is correct. For example, there have been instances of malicious edits of articles, such as the Seigenthaler incident mentioned on page 164. There have been spelling issues, as well as some unintentional inaccuracies that result from less-than-perfect knowledge of contributors. Wikipedia guidelines recommend that all articles have reliable sources, noting that "blogs, personal Web sites and Myspace don't count." Articles are encouraged to maintain a neutral point of view and are edited to eliminate bias. Although the "open to all" model should theoretically result in eventually removing all inaccuracies from entries, Wikipedia supplements this process by employing a dedicated editorial staff who can delete and improve material as well as insert reference sources where they are needed. Wikipedia also uses software robots to monitor and reverse obvious defacement of its articles.

Unlike other collections of information, such as encyclopedias, Wikipedia is not limited in size by the bounds of a print volume or specific topics. Because it is a user-created encyclopedia, Wikipedia's articles range far. Currently, Wikipedia has roughly 3 million articles in its English version, surpassing the number of entries in the *Brittanica* and Microsoft's Encarta. Wikipedia continues to grow at a rapid pace due to constant user contributions and currently has about 10 million articles in more than 200 languages. In fact, the *Britannica* has followed Wikipedia's lead and now allows users to contribute to its articles, although unlike the Wikipedia open-editing model, Britannica's contributions must go through a formal professional oversight process.

Wales has been living in St. Petersburg, Florida, since 2002. He has been married twice and has a daughter with his second wife, from whom he has separated.

(continued from page 166)
attention when she published a book about her decision to banish all screens—including televisions, desktop and laptop computers, cell phones, and iPods—from her life and the lives of her three teenage children for a nearly unthinkable six-month period. In *The Winter of Our Disconnect: How Three Totally Wired Teenagers (and a Mother Who Slept with Her iPhone) Pulled the Plug on Their Technology and Lived to Tell the Tale,* Ms. Maushart documents how although at first she experienced symptoms of withdrawal after turning off her iPhone, she and her family eventually rediscovered how to interact without relying on technological intermediaries and found that the world did not collapse in the process. Even for those who are unwilling or unable to take Ms. Maushart's half-year-long journey, it might be worthwhile and instructive to conduct a similar experiment for just one day to see where it leads.

CONCLUSIONS

Computers and the Internet have stretched the boundaries of one-to-one, one-to-many, and many-to-one communication beyond all previous limits. In fact, it can be hard to pigeonhole any form of Internet-based communication as one-to-one, one-to-many, or many-to-one. Although an e-mail message written by a single author may originally be intended to be read by one recipient and therefore be a one-to-one communication, such a message may soon find itself forwarded to a mailing list and quickly reach an audience of thousands, thereby becoming a one-to-many communication. Even e-mail messages written by Microsoft founder Bill Gates to a select few Microsoft employees later were uncovered as part of the antitrust investigation by Microsoft and became available for all the public to read. As another example, a blog entry that is in theory available to the world to read may in fact be lost among the millions of blog entries posted each day and therefore never read by anyone. In this way, a message intended to be one-to-many may in fact become one-to-one or even one-to-zero.

Furthermore, the ease of copying, modifying, and redistributing electronic information makes it possible not only to retransmit a message to someone other than its original recipient but also to change the message along the way. The sender of an e-mail message may be forged, making it appear to have been sent from someone other than its true author. Less perniciously, portions of digital music may be sampled, copied, and used as the basis for other songs. Video clips may be cut from movies and combined to form montages or parodies. News articles may be copied from online newspapers and then recut to create what appears to be an online magazine, but which contains articles selected to fit the tastes of a particular user. These are just a few ways in which what Professor Pamela Samuelson calls the plasticity of digital media is changing not only the way in which people communicate but the very nature of what it means to be an author or a reader, a composer or a listener, a filmmaker or a viewer. Now, with the Web still less than two decades old, designers and users of computer and Internet technology have only just begun to explore the ways in which technology can be used to expand and mold human communication.

CHRONOLOGY ───────

1439	Johannes Gutenberg invents mechanical printing press with movable type
1746	Abbé Jean-Antoine Nollet conducts experiment to discover how far and how quickly electricity can transmit information along wires
1793	Claude Chappe invents the first long-distance semaphore telegraph line
1809	Samuel Soemmering creates the first electrochemical telegraph
1825	William Sturgeon demonstrates the first electromagnet
1830	Joseph Henry discovers that electric current sent by wire could activate an electromagnet, causing a bell to strike
1831	Joseph Henry invents the first electric telegraph
1835	Samuel Morse invents Morse code
1843	Samuel Morse invents first electric telegraph line
	Alexander Bain patents the first fax machine
1861	East and West Coasts of America linked by telegraph wire
1866	Undersea telegraph cable connects the United States to England
1876	Thomas Edison patents the phonograph
1889	Almon Strowger patents the direct dial telephone
1894	Guglielmo Marconi greatly improves wireless telegraphy
1897	Cathode-ray tube invented, spurring the quest for the invention of television
1902	Guglielmo Marconi transmits radio signals across the Atlantic Ocean

1906	Lee De Forest invents the audion, which allows electronic signals to be amplified, improving telephones and radios
1914	The first telephone call is made across the Atlantic Ocean
	Belinograph, which closely resembles the modern fax machine, is invented
1916	Tuners added to radio sets, allowing different stations
1923	The first television is invented by Vladimir Kosma Zworykin
1925	John Logie Baird transmits the first television signal
1927	NBC creates two radio networks
	First television broadcast in England
1930	First television broadcast in the United States
	Golden Age of Radio begins
1933	FM radio invented
1941	First computers created
1951	Computers first sold commercially
1953	First color television sets available to consumers
1955	First fax sent across the North American continent
1969	ARPANET, the first Internet, is developed
1955	First e-mail sent
1976	Apple creates the first home computer
	First nationwide television station
	Project Gutenberg, an effort to digitize and archive cultural texts, started
1978	First multiplayer computer games developed
1979	Usenet developed
1981	First IBM PC sold

	Computer mouse becomes a regular part of the computer
	Cellular phone invented
1982	First e-mail sent across the Internet
1983	First cellular network created in the United States
1985	Car phone usage becomes widespread
1988	Fax machines capable of transmitting documents at 9,600 bits per second lead to tremendous growth in the use of faxes
1989	First commercial dial-up Internet access available
	Hypertext Transfer Protocol created
1991	First version of Linux operating system is distributed
1994	The Internet standard is made public
	WebCrawler, the first Web search engine, is created
	GeoCities Web site launches to enable easy creation of personalized Web pages and chat rooms, but fails to reach a critical mass, foreshadowing the rise of social networking sites more than a decade later
1995	Sun Microsystems releases Java programming language for creating software on all computer platforms
	Amazon online retailer launched
	eBay online auction service launched
	Craigslist founder Craig Newmark registers the domain name "craigslist.org" and begins posting San Francisco event announcements
	Classmates Web site launches to help people find and communicate with former schoolmates
1998	Satellite phone invented
	Google founded, Google search engine launched

2000	The dot-com bubble bursts, bankrupting many technology start-ups
2001	First e-mail sent to a mobile phone
	Wikipedia, a collaborative, online encyclopedia, is created
2002	U.S. Senator Trent Lott resigns after comments that he made praising segregation are picked up by bloggers and spread widely over the Internet
2003	Myspace, the first social network, is created
2004	Facebook is created
	Journalist Dan Rather broadcasts a story about President George W. Bush's National Guard service; bloggers discredit the documents on which the story is based, causing Rather to resign
2005	YouTube online video-sharing service launched
	The Huffington Post is launched as an alternative to print news media; by 2009 the site is listed second on *Time* magazine's list of the 25 best blogs of the year
2006	Google Docs free online collaboration software launched
	Twitter messaging and microblogging service launched
	The New Orleans Picayune runs a blog during Hurricane Katrina even while production of the print version of the newspaper is suspended, emphasizing the ability of blogs to break news of disasters in ways not possible with traditional print media
2007	Original iPhone released in the United States
	First generation iPod Touch released
	Amazon's first generation Kindle eBook reading device released
	Amazon MP3 digital music store launched beta version in the United States

Hulu's free online video service offers reruns of prime-time television shows and movies

2009   The reelection of Iranian President Mahmoud Admadinejad is covered widely by Web sites, blogs, and social networking sites, helping to expose corruption in the administration

2010   First Twitter message from the *International Space Station*

The New york Times begins to charge readers for unlimited access to the Web site

Google launches its Buzz social networking service in an attempt to compete with Facebook

Wikileaks releases 92,000 documents related to the war in Afghanistan to several major newspapers

2011   AOL acquires the Huffington Post for $135 million

Specific Media buys social networking company Myspace for $35 million, six years after News Corporation bought it for $580 million, showing the rapid decline of the company that first brought social networking to the masses

AOL acquires The Huffington Post—a news blog—for $315 million, making Arianna Huffington the president and editor-in-chief of all of AOL's media properties

Facebook, Twitter, and other social networking services play crucial role in "Arab Spring" uprisings in countries including Egypt, Libya, Bahrain, and Syria

GLOSSARY

Ajax   shorthand for Asynchronous JavaScript and XML; often used to enable content on webpages to change dynamically without requiring the entire page to reload

amplitude modulated (AM) radio   used in radio signals; varies the amplitude of the radio wave

assistive technology   users with disabilities can use assistive technology to regain function they have lost, like operating a computer

asynchronous communication   the transmission of data, often with a variable bitrate, that does not require synchronized timing signals on both ends of the transmission

audion   an electronic amplifying vacuum tube, used to detect audio signals and amplify them

bitmap   (as applied to fax images) the array of bits used to store information about digital images

block printing (printing press)   an early form of printing in which text and images are carved into a wooden block, which is then covered with ink and applied to a piece of cloth or paper

blog   shortened form of weblog; a Web site usually concentrating on a particular subject with entries in reverse chronological order

Bluetooth   wireless transmission technology for exchanging data over short distances

brick-and-mortar school   a traditional school housed in a physical building

chat room   any form of synchronous or asynchronous conferencing where messages are typically spontaneous and instantly visible

Child Online Protection Act (COPA)   a U.S. law restricting access by minors to harmful information on the Internet

177

chorded keyboard   a computer input device allowing users to type by pressing several keys at once, like playing a chord on a piano

client   computer hardware and/or software, which typically interacts directly with the user of a computer and which obtains services from a corresponding **server;** examples are e-mail clients, which allow users to send and receive e-mail messages transmitted over a network using an e-mail server, and Web browsers, which download webpages over the Internet from Web servers

client-server system   a system including a **client** and **server** of the same type; for example, a Web browser (client) and Web server make up a Web client-server system; in such a system, the client makes requests to the server for the server to provide information to the client or to perform actions on behalf of the client; in response to such requests, the server provides the request information to the client or performs the requested actions on behalf of the client

Communications Decency Act (CDA)   U.S. attempt to regulate pornography on the Internet; the law has been partially overturned

computer network   a collection of two or more computers connected in a way that enables them to transmit data

correspondence course   courses are offered online for students who are not able or would prefer not to attend a traditional lecture

crowdsourcing   the outsourcing of tasks or community projects to a large number of people who will most often do the work for free

cuneiform   one of the earliest forms of written communication, from Sumeria

customer relationship management (CRM)   modern software used by businesses to synchronize, organize, and automate common sales processes

desktop publishing (OTP)   the use of low-cost computers, software, printers, and the Internet to design and distribute books, newsletters, and other publications without the use of a traditional publishing company

desktop search software   allows you to search your computer and launch applications with a similar interface to popular Web searches

diploma mill   a for-profit educational institution, often in a foreign country, which confers advanced degrees with little or no required coursework, examinations, or requirements

distance education   allows students to participate in courses without attending a traditional classroom lecture

document management system   tracks and stores documents, typically records or content, for expedited retrieval

electronic document management (EDM)   a system of managing business data, also known as a **document management system**

e-mail   electronic mail, messages sent between people across the Internet

facsimile   a copy or a reproduction, facsimiles are created and sent electronically with a fax machine

fairness doctrine   a legal doctrine, promulgated by the U.S. Federal Communications Commission (FCC) from 1949–87, according to which radio and television broadcasts were required to provide balanced presentations of controversial issues of importance to the public

file server   a computer, typically with a very fast network connection, that is configured to send files to users who request them

frequency modulated (FM) radio   used in radio signals; varies the frequency of the radio wave

graphical user interface (GUI)   an interface that uses input devices like a mouse and keyboard in order to operate the computer

haptic technology   takes advantage of a user's sense of touch by applying forces, vibrations, or motions

hyperlink   clickable text that connects webpages, allowing users to navigate a Web site

HyperText markup language (HTML)   the language in which all webpages are encoded so that their text, graphics, and other content can be displayed properly by Web browsers

hypertext transfer protocol (HTTP)   the networking protocol that is at the foundation of the World Wide Web

illuminated manuscripts   a manuscript in which the text is decorated, such as by gold or silver

indecent speech   a category of speech protected by the First Amendment, but which the government has power to regulate on radio and television to protect children; the FCC has defined indecent speech as "language or material that, in context, depicts or describes, in terms patently offensive as measured by contemporary community standards for the broadcast medium, sexual or excretory organs or activities"

instant messaging (IM)   real-time chat sessions between users on the Internet

interactive voice response (IVR)   allows users to interact with the computer through voice commands using speech recognition technology

Internet radio   audio transmitted, typically in a continuous stream, across the Internet

Internet relay chat (IRC)   a popular protocol for real-time instant messaging and synchronous conferencing in chat rooms

local area network (LAN)   a network of computers near each other, such as in a home, school, or workplace

mail server   also known as a **mail transfer agent,** software that transfers electronic mail

mail transfer agent (MTA)   a synonym of **mail server**

mail user agent (MUA)   a computer program used to read a user's email

mainframe   a large and powerful data processing computer, typically located at a data center

message delivery agent (MDA)   software that is responsible for sending e-mail messages to a local user's mailbox

message transfer agent (MTA)   a synonym of **mail transfer agent**

mobile broadband   any type of high-speed Internet access through a portable modem or telephone, typically operating through satellite or cellular towers

modem   a device that modulates and demodulates a signal capable of being delivered across a telephone or cable line

movable type   a technology used in printing presses, in which individually movable pieces representing letters and other characters are arranged on a block to lay out a page of text for printing

Morse code   a code used to transmit data across telegraph wires

multimedia   media that uses more than one type of content, including text, audio, video, or interactive content

newsgroup   a repository of posted messages and information within the Usenet system

obscene speech   a type of speech that is not legally protected by the First Amendment; defined roughly as speech which appeals to the prurient interest, which describes sexual conduct in a patently offensive way, and which lacks serious literary, artistic, political, or scientific value

offset printing   an improvement to the original movable type printing process, in which an image is transferred from a plate to a rubber blanket and then to paper, instead of directly from the plate to paper

online auction   a Web site where users bid for products or services over the Internet

online course   a type of **correspondence course**

online degree program   a program offered by a university comprised entirely of **online courses**

online university   a university that offers only **online courses**

parallel cable   a cable capable of simultaneous transmission of data to and from each source

peer-to-peer network   a kind of computer network in which all computers in the network are connected to each other directly, rather than through a server

phonautograph   a device used to transcribe sound into a visible medium

post or **posting** a single entry on a blog; blog posts typically are listed in reverse chronological order

post office protocol (POP) the Internet standard protocol to receive e-mail from a remote server over a TCP/IP connection

printing press a machine that is used to print many copies of text by applying blank pages to a wooden or metal block of text

print server a computer or device connected to one or more printers as well as computers across a network, enabling the computers to send jobs to the printer remotely

prior restraint action taken by a government to prevent an individual or organization from engaging in speech before such speech has occurred, as in the case of a judicial order instructing a newspaper not to publish a particular article

public switched telephone network (PSTN) the network of telephone lines that allows any phone in the world to connect to any other phone

radar an object-detection system that uses radio waves to detect the presence, range, direction, and speed of objects

radio the transmission of a signal produced by oscillating electromagnetic fields

radiotelegraph the earliest form of the radio, essentially a telegraph machine that used radio waves instead of wires to carry a signal

really simple syndication (RSS) a Web standard that allows a Web site owner to aggregate a large amount of content, typically one or more **blogs,** for easy reading

router a networking device that enables incoming data packets to arrive at the right destination computer

satellite radio a digital radio signal relayed through satellites instead of traditional FM or AM stations

scarcity doctrine a legal doctrine, developed by the U.S. Supreme Court, according to which scarcity of the electromagnetic broadcast spectrum available for transmitting radio and television programs justifies the imposition of government restrictions on the speech contained within such programs, without violating the First Amendment

screen reader assistive technology, primarily for blind users, that reads aloud the contents of the screen

Semantic Web the group of standards and protocols that all computers are expected to support

semaphore means of conveying information across distances using optics; operators needed to be within visual or telescopic distance of a nearby tower

serial cable transfers data between two devices one bit at a time

server computer hardware and/or software that provides services to a **client** as part of a **client-server system;** examples of servers are **file servers** and **print servers**

short message service (SMS) the telecommunications standard that operates text messaging

simple mail transport protocol (SMTP) the Internet standard protocol to send email to a remote server over a TCP/IP connection

simulator a device that closely mimics some real thing, without the expense, risk, or other cons

sip/puff switch assistive technology used to send signals to a device by inhaling and exhaling on a straw or tube, primarily used by people who do not have the use of their hands

social networking an online platform where users can create profiles, connect with their friends, and share content

SOS the internationally recognized Morse code distress signal

speech recognition a technology that allows users to operate devices with their voice

state action a limitation of the First Amendment, and other parts of the U.S. Constitution, according to which only actions taken by government actors are prohibited by the First Amendment; private actors, such as private companies and universities, can censor speech of their employees and students without violating the First Amendment

subsequent punishment action taken by a government to punish an individual or organization for engaging in speech after such speech has occurred, as in the case of a fine imposed for publishing information about the location of troops during wartime

synchronous communication the transmission of data requiring each part of the system to be synchronized

switch a networking device that bridges together different segments of a network

telegraph a device that allowed long-distance transmission of electronic pulses

telephone a device that allowed long-distance transmission of voice data

television a device that allowed long-distance transmission of video

terminal a simple computing device, consisting of little more than a monitor, keyboard, and networking hardware, for connecting to a **mainframe** or other powerful computer; software running on the mainframe would provide output through the terminal's monitor, and the terminal's user could provide input the mainframe through the terminal's keyboard

text-to-speech synonym for **screen reader**

type a piece, often made out of wood or metal, representing an individual character for use with a movable type printing press

Universal Serial Bus (USB) a connectivity standard that allows devices to connect to any computer that supports USB connections

Usenet messages and posts collected in **newsgroups** and mirrored across all Usenet servers worldwide

user-generated content content created by individuals, instead of by professional agencies, like a personal blog or a YouTube video

Virtual Private Network (VPN) a data transfer standard that allows users to connect remotely and securely to a company's infrastructure

Voice over Internet Protocol (VoIP) a communication protocol that facilitates voice communications, like telephone calls, using the Internet instead of the traditional telephone network

Web 2.0   a term used to describe the high degree of interactivity, sharing, and community-centered development of modern Internet applications

Web services   a software system designed to support machine-to-machine interaction across a network

wide area network (WAN)   a computer network that covers a broad area, like a metropolis, region, or nation

wiki   a Web site that is built by the contributions of many individual users, instead of by a developer

Wireless N   the latest wireless networking standard in the 802.11 family

wireless network   two or more devices linked wirelessly, typically Wi-Fi, or the 802.11 standard

WYSIWYG   an acronym for "What You See Is What You Get," which refers to the ability of word processing and desktop publishing software to display documents in a form that closely resembles their appearance on the printed page, thereby eliminating the need to print a document to see how it will appear on paper

FURTHER RESOURCES

The following resources are arranged according to chapter title.

"History of Electronic Communication: From Morse Code to Talking through Your Computer"

BOOKS

Gearhart, Sarah. *The Telephone*. New York: Common Place Publishing, 1999. The story of the invention of the telephone and a discussion of how it revolutionized the world.

Gralla, Preston. *How Wireless Works*. Indianapolis, Ind.: Que Corporation, 2002. Explains how wireless data transmission works, including radios, televisions, remote controls, and cellular networks and what this means for data security and privacy in a world where anyone might be snooping.

Standage, Tom. *The Victorian Internet*. New York: Walker, 1998. The story of the rapid growth of the telegraph, and a cautionary tale of how new technologies inspire unrealistic hopes for universal understanding and peace.

ARTICLES

Bellis, Mary. "The History of the Telephone." About.com Web site. Available online. URL: http://inventors.about.com/od/bstartinventors/a/telephone.htm. Accessed June 23, 2011. An introduction to the origins of the telephone and how it rapidly became an important method of staying in touch.

Dunn, Julie. "Introduction and History of Modems." Dementia.org Web site. Available online. URL: http://www.dementia.org/~julied/tele2100/intro.html. Accessed June 23, 2011. The history of modems, and a description of how they work.

"Xerox at a Glance." Xerox.com Web site. Available online. URL: http://www.xerox.com/about-xerox/company-facts/enus.html. Accessed June 23, 2011. A fact sheet about Xerox, one of the largest names in enterprise and corporate printing, faxing, and copying supplies.

"Personal Communication: Staying in Touch with Friends and Family"

BOOKS

Davis, Jefferis. *Cyber Space.* New York: Crabtree Publishing Company, 1999. An exploration of consciousness and the nature of human intelligence through art, music, computer science, logic, and mathematics. An entertaining introduction to the relationship between computers and intelligent thought that does not require extensive mathematical knowledge and is accessible for the general reader.

ARTICLES

Metz, Cade. "Web 3.0." *PC Magazine* Web site. Available online. URL: http://www.pcmag.com/article2/0,2817,2102852,00.asp. Accessed June 23, 2011. This article addresses the question, "What will Web 3.0 look like?" In many ways, it is too soon to tell, but the article discusses how important people in the technology sector are helping shape the future of the Web.

"Online Activity Trends." Pew Research Center's Internet & American Life Project Web site. Available online. URL: http://www.pewinternet.org/Static-Pages/Trend-Data/Online-Activites-Total.aspx. Accessed June 23, 2011. This list of common activities shows how many Internet users use different services.

WEB SITES

Facebook. Available online. URL: http://www.facebook.com. Accessed June 23, 2011. Facebook is the world's largest social networking Web site.

Twitter. Available online. URL: http://www.twitter.com. Accessed June 23, 2011. Twitter allows users to send out micro-blogs, a maximum of 140 characters long, known as tweets.

"Business Communication: Beyond Interoffice Mail"

BOOKS

Gralla, Preston. *How the Internet Works.* Indianapolis, Ind.: Que Corporation, 2002. Explains the architecture of the Internet, including IP addresses, domain names, connectivity, and browsers.

Lowe, Doug. *Networking for Dummies.* Foster City, Calif.: IDG Books Worldwide, 1994. A technical reference book for local area networks, including printer sharing, building a network, and installing switches and routers.

ARTICLES

Beal, Vangie. "Understanding Web Services." Webopedia.com Web site. Available online. URL: http://www.webopedia.com/DidYouKnow/Computer_Science/2005/web_services.asp. Accessed June 23, 2011. A discussion of both old and new Web technologies.

"Voice over Internet Protocol." Federal Communications Commission (FCC) Web site. Available online. URL: http://www.fcc.gov/voip. Accessed June 23, 2011. Frequently asked questions about the Voice over Internet Protocol.

"Education: The Modern Classroom"

ARTICLES

"New Virtual Reality Surgery Simulator Hones Surgeons' Skills, Improves Patient Safety." Science Daily Web site. Available online. URL: http://www.sciencedaily.com/releases/2005/06/050627062144.htm. Accessed June 23, 2011. An extremely accurate simulation device allows surgeons to practice for many valuable hours on a video game before performing complex operations on patients.

WEB SITES

LeapFrog. Available online. URL: http://www.leapfrog.com/school. Accessed June 23, 2011. The LeapFrog platform allows children to learn through playing with a hand-held gaming console and educational games.

Project Explorer. Available online. URL: http://www.projectexplorer.org. Accessed June 23, 2011. This Web site allows students to select a foreign location they are interested in learning more about and view videos, recipes, history, and photographs from the area.

The Stock Market Game. Available online. URL: http://www.stockmarketgame.org. Accessed June 23, 2011. This education tool teaches children how the stock market works by teaching them how to trade using the same research and techniques professional stock traders use.

"Publishing and Journalism: The Printing Press Goes Online

BOOKS

Eisenstein, Elizabeth L. *The Printing Revolution in Early Modern Europe.* Cambridge: Cambridge University Press, 2005. Discusses technological innovation leading up to the printing press and how the invention of the Gutenberg press brought Europe into the modern era.

Keen, Andrew. *The Cult of the Amateur: How Blogs, Myspace, YouTube, and the rest of today's user-generated media are destroying our economy, our culture, and our values.* New York: Doubleday, 2007. Argues that Web 2.0 technologies, which enable anyone to become an author and publisher, are contributing to declining quality of creative works of all kinds.

ARTICLES

Carnoy, David L. "Self-publishing a Book: 25 Things You Need to Know." Cnet.com Web site. Available online. URL: http://reviews.cnet.com/self-publishing. Accessed June 23, 2011. The story of a CNet editor who decided to publish his own novel and the decisions he made along the way.

"Subsidy Publishing vs. Self-Publishing: What's the Difference?" Writing-World.com Web site. Available online. URL: http://www.writing-world.com/publish/subsidy.shtml. Accessed June 23, 2011. A useful guide for anyone considering publishing a book, either through a publisher or as a self-published work.

WEB SITES

Amazon. Available online. http://www.amazon.com. Accessed June 23, 2011. Amazon's Kindle e-book reader has yet to revolutionize the way people consume printed material, but the technology is still young.

The Huffington Post. Available online. http://www.huffingtonpost.com. Accessed June 23, 2011. The most successful newspaper and magazine alternative, the Huffington Post has over 3,000 bloggers and is one of the most popular Web sites on the Internet.

Lulu. Available online. http://www.lulu.com. Accessed June 23, 2011. Lulu allows writers to publish their own paperback books and receive royalties for every copy sold.

"Accessibility: Accommodating People with Disabilities"

BOOKS

Alliance for Technology Access. *Computer Resources for People with Disabilities.* Alameda, Calif.: Hunter House Publishers. 2004. A guide to assistive technologies, including new products, information specific to life situations, and tools for planning and decision-making about a new technology purchase.

ARTICLES

Curtis, Diane. "Disabled Bodies, Able Minds: Giving Voice, Movement, and Independence to the Physically Challenged." Edutopia Web site. Available online. URL: http://www.edutopia.org/assistivetechnology/. Accessed June 23, 2011. An introduction to how physically challenged people can recover many abilities through the use of assistive technology.

Filipus, Paul. "Computer Programmer and Analyst." American Foundation for the Blind CareerConnect Web site. Available online. URL: http://www.afb.org. Accessed June 23, 2011. A blind computer programmer uses assistive technologies to interact with a computer.

Gruber, John. "The iPad and Autism." Daring Fireball blog. Available online. URL: http://www.daringfireball.net. Accessed June 23, 2011. An examination of how the iPad might assist autistic individuals in communicating their thoughts, learning new life skills, and becoming engaged with, and through, the device.

WEB SITES

Better Living through Technology. Available online. http://www.bltt.org/. A Web site that offers impartial information and ideas on the use of assistive technology.

RehabTool. Available online. http://www.rehabtool.com/. A Web site specializing in computer adaptation and custom software solutions for children and adults with disabilities.

"Freedom of Speech: Is There Anything You Cannot Say?"

ARTICLES

"Enemies of the Internet." Reporters without Borders Web site. Available online. URL: http://www.ifex.org/international/2010/03/12/internet_

enemies.pdf. Accessed June 23, 2011. A list of the countries that most suppress online expression.

Glanville, Jo. "The Big Business of Net Censorship." Guardian.co.uk Web site. Available online. URL: http://www.guardian.co.uk/commentisfree/2008/ nov/17/censorship-internet. Accessed June 23, 2011. An article detailing who has the most to gain and lose from net neutrality, proprietary Internet, and censorship.

Smith, David. "Timeline: A History of Free Speech." Guardian.co.uk Web site. Available online. URL: http://www.guardian.co.uk/media/2006/feb/05/ religion.news. Accessed June 23, 2011. This chronology follows the evolution of the right to free speech, from Ancient Greece to recent court cases.

"The Universal Declaration of Human Rights." United Nations Web site. Available online. URL: http://www.un.org/en/documents/udhr. Accessed June 23, 2011. The Universal Declaration of Human Rights, drafted after the end of World War II, cites the freedom of speech as a fundamental human right.

WEB SITES

ACLU Online Free Speech. Available online. http://www.aclu.org/free-speech/online-free-speech. The ACLU Online Free Speech library follows legal cases related to the freedom of online speech.

"From One-to-One to Many-to-Many: The Wide Reach of Computer Communication"

BOOKS

Rheingold, Howard. *Virtual Communities: Homesteading on the Electronic Frontier.* Reading, Mass.: Addison-Wesley Publishing Company, 1993. Available online. URL: http://www.rheingold.com/vc/book. Written in 1993, this was one of the earliest texts about the Internet.

ARTICLES

Bell, Genevieve, and Dourish, Paul. "Yesterday's Tomorrows: Notes on Ubiquitous Computing's Dominant Vision." Journal of Personal and Ubiquitous Computing, 2007. Available online. URL: http://portal.acm.org/citation. cfm?id=1229069. Accessed June 23, 2011. This article explores the vision of ubiquitous computing pioneers and the contemporary practice that has emerged.

Doheny-Farina, Stephen. "Default=Offline Or Why Ubicomp Scares Me." Computer-Mediated Communication Magazine. Available online. URL: http://www.december.com/cmc/mag/1994/oct/last.html. Accessed June 23, 2011. This article formulates four rules that must be followed for ubiquitous computing to be successful while maintaining user privacy.

Liu, Alan. "To the Student: Appropriate Use of Wikipedia." University of California, Santa Barbara Web site. Available online. URL: www.english.ucsb.edu/faculty/ayliu/courses/wikipedia-policy.html. Accessed June 23, 2011. A description of the drawbacks of Wikipedia, or any crowd-sourced effort, including unreliability and vandalism.

Niles, Robert. "A Journalist's Guide to Crowdsourcing." Online Journalism Review. Available online. URL: http://www.ojr.org/ojr/stories/070731niles/. Accessed June 23, 2011. Some examples of how a journalist uses crowdsourcing to find news stories.

INDEX

Italic page numbers indicate illustrations.

A

abbreviations, in online communications 41

academic portals 87–88

accessibility xvi–xvii, 121–137, *126, 128, 132*

adaptive and alternative keyboards 123–124

Admadinejad, Mahmoud 175

advertising, in news 111

Ajax 52

Amazon 22, 25–28, 66–67, 70, 174, 175

Amazon Kindle *113,* 114, 175

American Radio and Research Company (AMRAD) 15

amplitude modulated (AM) radio 15

Anderson, Tom 49

antennas, on televisions 18

AOL Instant Messenger (AIM) 40–41

Apollo Group, Inc. 97

Arab Spring 176

Armstrong, Edwin Howard 15

ARPANET 36, 52, 173

Ars Minor 79

assistive technology. *See* accessibility

asynchronous communication 21, 90

AT&T 11, 34, 46–47

Auction Web 76

audion 14, 173

autism 133

automated clearing house (ACH) 72

automation, in customer relations 69–70

B

Bain, Alexander 11, 172

Baird, John 17, 173

bandwidth, broadcast 142, *143*

Barger, Jorn 42

Barlow, John Perry 146–150

Bauerlein, Mark 166

Beeson, Ann *148,* 148–150

Belin, Édouard 11

Belinograph 11, 173

Bell, Alexander Graham 7–8, *8,* 32

bill payment, online 71–72

binary files 42

bitmaps, in fax transmission 12

Blackboard Inc. 87–88

block printing 101

Blogger 43

blogs xvi, 42–46, *44,* 66, 107–108, 151

Bluetooth 28

Bolt, Beranek and Newman (BBN) 36, 51–52

Book of Kells 101

books, electronic 110, 112–118, 173

Braille 125, *126,* 129–130

Brainerd, Paul 105

broadband modems 24–25, 38–39

broadcast bandwidth 142, *143*

Buccos, Jenny M. 83

Bulletin Board Systems (BBSs) 40, 49

Bush, George W. 175

business communication xvi, 6–7, 56–78, *65*

business-to-business communication 72–77